Spiritual Friendship

Christian Morgenstern, December 1913

Spiritual Friendship

Rudolf Steiner
and
Christian Morgenstern

Peter Selg

SteinerBooks | 2018

SteinerBooks
An imprint of Anthropsophic Press, Inc.
610 Main St., Great Barrington, MA 01230
www.steinerbooks.org

 Originally published in German as *Geistige Hilfeleistung: Rudolf Steiner und Christian Morgenstern* (Verlag des Ita Wegman Instituts, 2014).

Text translated by Marsha Post
Poetry translated by Christopher Bamford

This volume was made possible by a generous gift from a donor who wishes to remain anonymous

Translator's note: Because the poems in this volume are of a very special nature (as you will soon read), they cannot simply be translated directly and retain their full essence. Ideally, they live in our hearts and souls in such a way that one day they could reincarnate into our own language. Therefore, what is given here is a somewhat a literal translation of each poem in prose, accompanied by the original text in German.

Library of Congress Control Number: 2018936127
ISBN: 978-1-62148-222-2 (paperback)
ISBN: 978-1-62148-223-9 (ebook)

Printed in the United States of America

Contents

Gesegnet ging ich in die Welt,
mein Land von Deiner Hand bestellt.

Wie oft seitdem, als Trostespfand,
erschien mir diese liebe Hand –

und schrieb in meine Viergestalt
ihr Kreuz wie einen stillen Halt.

2/3 V. 12.

Handwritten poem by Christian Morgenstern for Rudolf Steiner,
Arosa, Switzerland, May 2/3, 1912

For Sergei O. Prokofieff

The higher an individual rises in self-development and therefore is firm in one's own "I," the more that one possesses the capability to bring toward a still higher being the full recognition, yes, a free, open recognition, because the honoring is founded in knowledge. This was the kind of honor Christian Morgenstern had in relation to his friend and teacher Rudolf Steiner, an honor that bore in itself absolute sovereignty, independence and naturalness.... One almost wishes to say: I can hardly imagine anything more beautiful or that points more to the future than the spiritual friendship between Rudolf Steiner and Christian Morgenstern.

Sergei O. Prokofieff[1]

Foreword

I published the comprehensive book *Christian Morgenstern: Sein Weg mit Rudolf Steiner* [Christian Morgenstern: His path with Rudolf Steiner] to document Christian Morgenstern's relationship to Anthroposophy, building on foundational preparatory work by Michael Bauer, Margareta Morgenstern, Rudolf Meyer, Christopher Rau, Hella Wiesberger, and Reinhardt Habel. It was published by Verlag Freies Geistesleben in Stuttgart.

This study arose from preparatory lectures for the Morgenstern Memorial Year in 2014 (he died March 31, 1914) and focuses on that Memorial Year. In view of the epochal anniversary of the beginning of World War I and the events, questions, and excitement with which it is connected, it seems important not to lose sight of the witnessing and commitment of Morgenstern (a model anthroposophist). Christian Morgenstern tried to recommend Rudolf Steiner to receive the Nobel Peace Prize in 1913/14 (with a detailed and relevant foundation of such interest that it is still worth reading today). He also had at his disposal a decisive acquaintance with Anthroposophy and with Rudolf Steiner's being and work. The view for the civilizational situation and the actual practice of anthroposophical esotericism belong together within the objectives of the

Independent School for Spiritual Science and the General Anthroposophical Society. "We have to recognize that the task will come to our Society in particular to unite the greatest public openness with genuine, true esotericism."[2]

Christian Morgenstern's way of working with Anthroposophy from 1909 to 1914 was, and remains, substantially significant for Rudolf Steiner and the progress of the anthroposophical movement on Earth. According to Rudolf Steiner, the effects of his selfless penetration of the newly revealed spiritual treasure with clear thinking and devotion reached far beyond Christian Morgenstern himself, and following his death it continues to work objectively today in the spiritual world. Steiner's presentations of this fact can lead to a deep insight into the spiritual work and inner transformation he had hoped for from his esoteric pupils, showing why he was so grateful to Morgenstern. Rudolf Steiner never wished for endless expressions of gratitude toward himself, nor did he want gifts or personal devotion. The assistance he needed for the progress of anthroposophical affairs lay in a different realm. For thirty-three years, Sergei O. Prokofieff was active in this realm in an exemplary way. This study is dedicated to him and his work for the future.[3]

Peter Selg
Ita Wegman Institute, Arlesheim
Holy Nights 2013/14

Introduction

Everything that is happening serves the future.
Everything is preparation.
Everything past serves the future.[4]

Meetings between Christian Morgenstern and Rudolf Steiner extended over a period of nearly five years—from January 28, 1909, in Berlin until January 2, 1914, in Leipzig.[5] Christian Morgenstern was able to speak privately several times with Rudolf Steiner. In 1909, he spoke with Steiner in Christiania (Oslo), Kassel, and Munich. Their longest conversation together took place three years later in a Zürich hotel room. During their conversation, he gave Rudolf Steiner unpublished poems from his forthcoming volume, *We Have Found a Path*. Their final conversations took place in Stuttgart in November 1913 and in Leipzig at the turn of the year from 1913 to 1914, three months before Morgenstern's death.

However, even beyond their meetings and conversations, a continuous relationship developed between the two individualities. For more than five years, Christian Morgenstern followed the development of Rudolf Steiner's work with great intensity, including Steiner's published writings, his lecture courses (some of which Morgenstern had attended or read later), as well as Steiner's Mystery Dramas performed in Munich. The extremely conscious and concentrated performances of these epochal works were, without a doubt, central events of Christian Morgenstern's last five years of life and creative activity, and he described it as such. In reviewing his biography, he saw that it had been directed toward this time and that it's arrival had been long in preparation: "Your path leads you."[6] In short prose texts, poems, letters, and personal lines to Rudolf Steiner (some as dedications of his books), he expressed this in an impressive way, filled with "unending gratitude" (Marie Steiner-von Sivers[7]). "This gave his eye its particular shine, a radiant glow of mildness and goodness..."[8]

Rudolf Steiner's experience of Christian Morgenstern's entry to the theosophical–anthroposophical movement is not documented in detail—unless we consider the various indications in his introductory words before poetry readings (during Morgenstern's life in Stuttgart and Leipzig) and in memorial addresses following his death. Christian Morgenstern needed and received Rudolf Steiner's spiritual help for the increasing fulfillment of his life and work. His nature, his poetry, and above all his special, unique way of working with Anthroposophy was also tremendously significant for Rudolf Steiner, though the significance is far more difficult to recognize. Despite the maturity and greatness of Morgenstern's individuality, the relationship between spiritual teacher to esoteric pupil remained intact throughout his life. Nonetheless, Rudolf Steiner loved Morgenstern in his lofty spirituality, in the purity of his soul, and in his special form of being, about which Morgenstern commented in two rare personal statements in the following words:

> Above all, however, people such as me are needed from time to time; otherwise, the mysterious character of the Earth, the world, and life would be forgotten.... Of course, many people talk about it but, to experience it passionately and to express it fully, this painful grace is probably reserved for and offered to only a few. Now, I do not want to make the final judgment about me with these words. I sincerely hope and believe that my body will fall apart more than my mind, and then everything is fine.[9]
>
> I have a feeling of boldness about my whole life, as if my path often went past the hedge of Paradise. Then a warm breeze touches me and I believe I am seeing and smelling roses, and a sweet tone moves me to tears and rests for just a moment on my brow as a loving, peace-bestowing hand. Therefore, I often walk past the hedge of Paradise.[10]

Following Morgenstern's death, Rudolf Steiner outlined the special circumstances of the path "past the hedge of Paradise" to members of the Anthroposophical Society who felt closely connected inwardly with Christian Morgenstern. At a memorial for the dead in Kassel, among other things Rudolf Steiner said:

> The way Christian Morgenstern came to terms with his earthly incarnation shows us how his soul strove from spiritual heights to find the incarnation most appropriate for this special individuality. We saw in him a soul that could not bring itself to conform fully to the strong materialistic life that prevailed from the late nineteenth century into the early twentieth century. We might say that, through incarnation, his soul imposed a certain restraint on itself. In a sense, he was holding back some of his soul forces—keeping them back in the spiritual world. Looking at the earthly world, he was always fully aware of the perspective that comes from being rooted halfway in the spiritual world.

Thus, Christian Morgenstern could hardly have found a lineage more suitable for him than that of his ancestors, who were painters. His father was a painter from a family of painters. His family had developed a habit of looking at what the earthly sphere offers from the perspective of a spiritually oriented artist. From a spiritually minded, artistic perspective his family loved all the beauty of nature and all the beauty that can flower from human life, even when it's basis is materialistic.

This is how Christian Morgenstern was placed into a lineage that led to the development of a certain connection in him to nature; he came from a family of landscape painters. In other words, he was endowed with a special relationship to nature that was strengthened further and expanded from early childhood, when his parents took him with them on their frequent travels. The impulse to create poetry awoke in him at an early age as he was growing up. We can observe, then, how he developed this poetic impulse in subsequent years; we might say that, in his soul life, he withdrew to a desert island and viewed the world around him from the vantage point of that island.

During those early years, poems poured from his poetic soul. Delicate verses were born from a soul that remained partly rooted in the spiritual realm. Other verses poured out, too. When we look into the poet's soul more closely, we can understand that those other verses originated in the same soul from which those delicate verses arose. We can understand the source and purpose of those other verses, which express all the disharmony we encounter in outer life in our present age. This is why, in addition to poems that soar upward in a prayerful mood, Christian Morgenstern also composed other verses that are more well known to the outer world. Indeed, those biting, ironic, and humorous poems that such a soul must breathe out are just about the only ones of his extensive work that the

> outer world knows. Just as our physical lungs, after inhaling fresh air, must exhale carbon dioxide permeated air, such a soul must exhale such poems. In this twofold respiratory process of the spiritual life, the poet's soul had to rise prayerfully to the most exalted wisdom and beauty of life and the world. It also had to look at everything unnatural and artificial and at the discrepancies and disharmony of the surrounding world, which must have been especially obvious and disturbing for such a spiritually minded soul. Thus he felt compelled to resort to slight, fleeting humor to rise above and laugh away the world's discrepancies.
>
> Christian Morgenstern is sure to be remembered as one of those artists who shows us so clearly how deeply linked a prayerful mood is to light humor. This connection is especially close in a spiritually minded soul such as that of Christian Morgenstern. Indeed, it was through the prayerful tone of his poems—what soared upward to a prayerful mood—that Christian Morgenstern was predestined to join his path in life with the life path of our spiritual movement.[11]

Rudolf Steiner therefore merely intimated Morgenstern's "special individuality" and its similarly special circumstances of incarnation at the turn of the nineteenth to twentieth century. Through incarnation, according to Steiner, his individuality laid upon itself a "certain restraint...*as it were, to remain with certain forces back in the spiritual world and always to view the earthly world fully imbued with the viewpoint that arises when one is halfway rooted in the spiritual world.*" Morgenstern followed his path in this way from childhood on. He was an astute observer and critic of materialism in all of its contemporary manifestations. Yes, he was a real and extremely productive "witness of the times." Nevertheless, beyond his poetry, he was able to intervene actively only partially in his time. His illness, but more so the whole signature of his earthly existence (including the illness), prevented him from doing so. In his "seraphic joy" (Rudolf Meyer[12]) and Platonic mood,[13] Morgenstern remained a guest on Earth, but at the same time was a man who suffered through his destiny completely before his individuality left the earthly body and, five months before the outbreak of the murderous World War I, returned to the spiritual world. Looking back at a meeting in Zürich with Christian Morgenstern in late September 1912, one-and-a-half years before the death of the poet, Rudolf Steiner said:

> At the time, the deterioration of his body had advanced to such a degree that he could not speak above a whisper. Something lived in Christian Morgenstern's soul, however, that made outer speech almost unnecessary, even for the physical plane.... The unique language that spoke from his eyes spoke with such intimacy.... Christian Morgenstern's sweet, intimate smile radiated like a beacon as if from the spiritual world.[14]

Rudolf Steiner was also extremely warm toward other coworkers in the Anthroposophical Society and movement. He occasionally thanked them effusively for their commitment to Anthroposophy and, insofar as they were productive, praised (often effusively) and repeatedly drew attention to their work. Nonetheless, his inner relationship to Christian Morgenstern was, without a doubt, special. Steiner not only introduced Morgenstern's poetry in Stuttgart and Leipzig, but he also said in his Stuttgart address on November 24, 1913 (three months before the friend's death):

> Since I can speak to you quite personally for a few moments, allow me to make this remark. I would often have the feeling that there is some person within our movement who, for one reason or another, has an impulse to make someone happy. It is always a personal joy for me when many souls in our movement have deepened themselves through what can be achieved in this area—when many souls are able to turn to a proper, true, clear reception of Morgenstern's poetry. Moreover, if I should speak of the joy that one or another wants to give me personally, such individuals can do this best by showing themselves willing to penetrate with understanding what we now want to give you as several good examples. These are the things through which we may feel personally connected with our movement, while at the same time may, so to speak, step out of our roles and speak intimately and personally of our joy. We may say that the greatest of these joys is connected with the fact that we have in our midst a poet such as Christian Morgenstern.[15]

In Leipzig, after the introduction of Christian Morgenstern's poem (on New Year's Eve Day 1913), Rudolf Steiner took the roses from the vase beside his lectern, walked the full length of a hall in Hôtel de Pologne and gave them to Christian Morgenstern, who was sitting in the last row, and hugged him. Three months later, he arranged the entire cremation ceremony for the deceased friend and, according to Marie Steiner-von Sivers, stood at his grave and wept, overflowing with tears. "We were in pain over his physical end... because we loved him so much."[16]

At this point, however, the closeness between Christian Morgenstern and Rudolf Steiner (or, rather, between their individualities) had in no way ended. Indeed, their relationship attained the next and even more intensive stage, as

Rudolf Steiner pointed out repeatedly in the year following Morgenstern's death on March 31, 1914. With the following words, he also indicated what the spiritual friend in the realms of heaven signifies for the future of Anthroposophy:

> Light's weaving essence, it gleams
> from human to human
> to fill the whole world with truth.
> Love's blessing, it warms
> the soul to soul,
> weaving the redemption of all worlds.
> And spirit messengers wed
> people's works of blessing
> with world goals.
> And if the two can unite,
> then those who find their self in humanity
> radiate spirit light through warmth of soul.
>
> *Des Lichtes webend Wesen, es erstrahlet*
> *Von Mensch zu Mensch*
> *Zu füllen alle Welt mit Wahrheit.*
> *Der Liebe Segen, er erwarmet*
> *Die Seele an der Seele,*
> *Zu wirken aller Welten Seligkeit*
> *Und Geistesboten, sie vermählen*
> *Der Menschen Segenswerke*
> *Mit Weltenzielen;*
> *Und wenn vermählen kann die beiden*
> *Der Mensch, der sich im Menschen findet,*
> *Erstrahlet Geisteslicht durch Seelenwärme.*[17]

Christian Morgenstern, 1910

I

"Your Cross as a Silent Support"

The significance of Rudolf Steiner for Christian Morgenstern

Christian Morgenstern had special, discerning sight and a special ability to perceive and understand Rudolf Steiner's Anthroposophy and the tasks and goals that would remain connected to it. Morgenstern's remarkable "sight" had to do not only with the extent, or stage, of his individuality's development and distinctive sensibility, but also with the path of suffering he experienced before encountering anthroposophical Spiritual Science. Struggling in a sick earthly body, he endured and experienced the materialism at the end of the nineteenth century and the harsh distress of the soul and spirit connected with it. He lived through the abyss and drama of "not knowing," and after many years thus attained organs of compassion. Christian Morgenstern did not encounter, as so many born after him, the full collection of Rudolf Steiner's works, and so he inwardly endured and suffered on his own through countless "answers" to the questions he experienced. Instead, he met Rudolf Steiner late in his life, after a long inner journey. In a retrospective observation that was both serious and full of humor, he said of his education:

> I have to thank myself, several private individuals, and chance for almost all that I have become. I felt no conscious, organic culture around me that could have educated or systematically trained a single individual. Neither parents nor teachers or anyone else took me strongly in hand to educate me in any real sense. Moreover, if I—a human being of original brilliance—have remained, on the whole, a dilettante, half the blame for it goes to the enormous degree of amateurishness, halfheartedness, and a lack of culture I found wherever my eventful youth has taken me.[18]

At the age of twenty-one (at the end of his third seven-year period), Morgenstern noted in his diary: "Oh, that I would find someone who understands me and who would guide me in certain things; the loneliness of rising upward is terrible."[19] Morgenstern went through much searching—not through the errors of life, but through the realm of spiritual uncertainty and without access to the truth, the true "I," and to the spirituality of the world. "Creation remained, as always, a unique and tragic incomprehensibility, understandable to the feeling but impenetrable for the mind, offering little more than thoughts of despair to a great will."[20] After years of spiritual effort, he finally found his way to Anthroposophy through the eye of the needle of John's Gospel, "opening through John."[21] This way led through the initiated pupil of Jesus Christ, the Evangelist and writer of the Apocalypse (and later leader of the Rosicrucian community), to the movement he recognized as the bearer of the new Logos Mysteries.[22]

In Anthroposophy, Christian Morgenstern saw the dawn and beginning of the next cultural epoch and stage. With great devotion and wakefulness, he studied spiritual-scientific knowledge of the human being and Christology, the newly opened access to the world of the living through Anthroposophy, and the development of culture and consciousness. *"I understand absolutely that, first and foremost, nothing counts except learn, learn, learn!"*[23]

Morgenstern was not a naïve beginner and was not prone to exaggerated devotion or fanaticism. After his examination of Anthroposophy—against the burden of prejudices and alienations—he recognized a spiritual and spiritually momentous new beginning in it, a fundamental new impact in human evolution and a real "future movement...*a pure and undivided acceptance of the great, significant new human.*"[24] This was obvious to him in that moment, as he saw and experienced the "Great New Thing." He was not hindered by the "nonsense" (or "fools") in the Theosophical, and later the Anthroposophical Society, that existed within the circle of worshipers surrounding Rudolf Steiner, as is the case around every great or renowned individuality. Nor was he impeded by the incomprehension of his closest friends.

Christian Morgenstern's intense, unrelenting struggle with those friends can be seen against this background (expressed in greatest detail by his relationship with Friedrich Kayssler,[25] but certainly not limited to him). Morgenstern could not and would not accept the opinion that the true spirit of Rudolf Steiner and Anthroposophy should remain inaccessible to the best of his spiritually seeking companions. They did not let this being approach them at all, but instead hid themselves in a fortress of preconceptions (and negative presentiments), and thus completely neglected the reality of contemporary Spiritual Science. Friedrich Kayssler was an excellent actor and connoisseur of modern theater. When Morgenstern asked him to read the text of Rudolf Steiner's first Mystery Drama, *The Portal of Initiation,* he turned away in astonishment after a brief look, which Morgenstern was unwilling to accept.

> Steiner's mystery... is not just a *play;* rather, it *reflects* the spiritual worlds and truths. Although it may have some of the difficulties of a beginning work or first effort, it introduces a new stage and epoch of art. That epoch itself remains distant; it could be hundreds of years before people who want this pure spiritual art become so numerous that mysteries of this kind can be offered and accepted in almost every city. Nevertheless, its historical beginning, when we experience its birth, is here in the "Portal."[26]

A few months before his death, Morgenstern wrote to his deeply religious friend Marie Goettling (the daughter of a pastor from Sorau), who was entirely unreceptive to Rudolf Steiner's Christology, with which she did not wish to even acquaint herself, and who took exception to the superficiality of the theosophical movement:

> Take a look at today's world and compare it to your youth. Add another fifty or eighty years, and the wasteland will have spread so much that one would no longer wish to live, unless there were at least islands of spiritual life—unless a disappearing minority worked in advance for this. That is the assistance we can give. Such help and its tragic necessity, which you apparently refuse to understand, that is the Christianity calling today, about which the official Church and numerous proponents of a private, personal Christianity (in light of the Church's opinion), wish to know

> very little. Do you not see that something here is dying and must be replaced by something new? There is a *new Christian work,* because the old is no longer enough, and a *nova vita* [new life] must intervene for the followers of Christ. This fresh new start does not involve merely being good and doing good, but must, in addition, turn to measures that evolution offers and only the proper cultivation of which can prevent, so that the good and best will not finally end in despair.
>
> One must always speak only partially about oneself, but I must say that I do not know where I would be today if the insights of Theosophy had not made life understandable and bearable for me—perhaps in despair, in madness, in revolution somewhere, in philistinism, perhaps nowhere on this side of the grave.[27]

None of the students surrounding Rudolf Steiner and no members of the Anthroposophical Society during the first decades of the twentieth century were willing to wrestle with old friends over Anthroposophy in a way that even comes close to what Morgenstern experienced as documented and revealed in letters. Christian Morgenstern did not, in any way, have a missionary's disposition. Nevertheless, he remained strongly loyal to his friends and previous comrades, and because of this friendship and high regard he also tried to bring them to a path—*his* path—or at least introduce them to it. "My greatest pain remains that I set out on this new path *without you.*"[28] He wrote in one of his notebooks. "Let go of no one; drop no relationship."[29]

Morgenstern was certainly not concerned only with the spiritual welfare of his friends, who were mostly virtuous and exhibited no difficulties in this regard, but rather concerned about their about missing—like so many others—the turning point of spiritual world history, which Morgenstern considered to be the appearance and effectiveness of anthroposophic Spiritual Science. Something immensely great and new in its very first beginning and initial entry to culture was mocked, condemned, or ignored—mostly all three. Rudolf Steiner often pointed out the need for patience, leniency, and forbearance with the slow acceptance of Anthroposophy in the contemporary reality of society and the world. In Berlin, at the first General Meeting on February 4, 1913, he said:

> People will learn how deeply what we present as Anthroposophy and what we receive through Anthroposophy is substantiated in the human being, for it is our being. This being hovered close to humans to show itself as a heavenly goddess, with whom the human being could enter a relationship, and who lived as Sophia, or *Philosophia*. Human beings will again set this being outside themselves and recognize in it a reflection of the human being. We will set it before us as the result of true self-knowledge in Anthroposophy. We can wait confidently until the world wishes to examine what we have to say and how deeply substantiated it is in every detail; the being of Anthroposophy—its own being—consists of what the being of the human is. That is the nature of its effectiveness; human beings receive what they actually are in Anthroposophy and must place it before themselves, because they must practice self-knowledge.[30]

In this, Christian Morgenstern agreed completely with Rudolf Steiner. He also saw (as did his spiritual teacher and friend) the dilemma of the time and the disastrous dynamic of the evolution of civilization. He was the only student and coworker of Rudolf Steiner who tried to introduce Steiner's life's accomplishments and work to the broader public, which at this point was in no way finished or even at its peak.

Moreover, he did not do this through his poetry but through a petition to the Nobel Prize committee. Michael Bauer, his best and most advanced anthroposophical friend, once said about it that it was still impossible for Rudolf Steiner's students and colleagues to recognize his full significance. He said, "We are standing too close to 'see' him."[31] Christian Morgenstern saw this too, yet he was in a position, like Bauer, to perceive the world-historic relevance and impact of Anthroposophy, even in the hour of its beginning, as well as the significance of Anthroposophy and the significance of Rudolf Steiner, who brought and placed it into scientific and cultural history at the beginning of the twentieth century. He probably formulated the first draft of his letter to the Nobel Prize Committee during the second half of 1913, following a performance of the fourth Mystery Drama in Munich. Among other things he wrote:

> The man to whom I wish to bring your attention in all modesty is Dr. Rudolf Steiner, the inaugurator of the present anthroposophical movement in Central Europe. To one who has known this movement intimately for years, Dr. Rudolf Steiner fulfills the conditions of the Nobel Prize in three ways: as a scientist, as a poet, and as an advocate of peace. Aside from the fact that his main philosophical work, *The Philosophy of Freedom*, must be recognized as the most important production of modern German philosophy; apart from his many writings on Goethe, which include his introductions to Goethe's natural scientific works in the Kürschner National Literature that deserve a place of excellence; and, finally, apart from his newly and completely revised edition of *The Riddles of Philosophy*, Rudolf Steiner—as the author of *Christianity as Mystical Fact, Theosophy, How to Know Higher Worlds*, and *An Outline of Esoteric Science*, to name the

most comprehensive books—is the first spiritual-scientific scholar and author of Europe, and yes, one must go further and say, the first of our whole present-day culture. If it is possible for those who are outsiders to check these facts, so must they conclude from the records that Rudolf Steiner has a significant and special standing as a poet. The four great Mystery Dramas he has given so far to anthroposophists already presuppose anthroposophical life.

It is not the intention of the undersigned to speak here of Rudolf Steiner as a phenomenon of science or of poetry, but only to speak of his third characteristic—as one of the *greatest supporters of world freedom.* Indeed, if anyone is working to bring people together in brotherhood, it is this man, who alone through his personality gets people of different nationalities to unite in the most noble spiritual striving. Even more, the manner and content of the teaching he has developed, cultivated, and spread untiringly for the past ten years are more permanent than what he could manage through his personality. Much of this teaching can be received from the books named here. The actual activity of Rudolf Steiner, in the most noble sense of humanity, will nonetheless be discovered only by historians who are called to write the story of this noble life. Then one will perceive with deep amazement what was and is being done quietly for human beings as such, as well as the irreplaceable support and foundation the life work of this spirit has given as the century speeds increasingly into the terrible wasteland of materialism.

It would be a point of light so important for us all if it would be possible for you, most honorable gentlemen, to turn your attention to this high human figure of our day, and, on my word of honor, I deem it necessary to assure you (to prevent from the beginning any later misunderstanding) that I have never spoken to Rudolf Steiner or to any person close to him about the Nobel Prize. I have also

> not received any prompting from him or any member of the Anthroposophical Society for my idea.
>
> My impulse for this arises freely from my own personal initiative and not from my capacity as an anthroposophist. It comes merely from my being as a German author, following thorough consideration of what my recommendation will face. How much underestimation, misjudgment, yes, disavowal...[32]

At this point, the draft of the letter breaks off permanently—probably not completely by accident. It was found later in Morgenstern's estate. Whether he wrote a second version is unknown. The process was remarkable in any case; beyond this, Morgenstern's presentation of reasons for the Nobel Peace Prize was given at a time when the General Anthroposophical Society had not yet been founded in its worldwide unifying power, and at a time when the laying of the Foundation Stone for the Independent School for Spiritual Science in Dornach was only a wish (to which people from all the nations should come in the second half of the twentieth century).

Morgenstern's basis for recommending the Nobel Peace Prize was justified and demonstrated the foresight and comprehensive knowledge of the contemporary who recognized Rudolf Steiner's task and work early and with a succinct clarity. This was decades before the beginning of the fanatical racism of materialistic nationalism, the politics of destruction, euthanasia, the Holocaust, and the atomic bomb. Morgenstern saw clearly the potential and prospects for the whole of civilization and for the inner path of the individual that is connected with the knowledge of the human being in the light of Anthroposophy. "*What was and is being done quietly for human beings as such, as well as what irreplaceable support and foundation the life work of this spirit has given as the century speeds ever further into the terrible wasteland of materialism.*" And yet, "How much underestimation, misjudgment, yes, disavowal..."

In another, somewhat autobiographical text that Christian Morgenstern wrote at the urging of his publisher Reinhard Piper for an almanac, he said about Rudolf Steiner:

> In Rudolf Steiner, a person came among us who signifies something entirely new for the evolution of the human soul. In a certain sense, he closed the history of philosophy that comprises a long discipline of pure exoteric thinking, and he founded—not as the absolutely first person, but as the first philosopher and the first scholar and researcher—Spiritual Science, which views the human as a cosmic being: Anthroposophy. Because of him and his research, even the most independent person can reflect and revise anew. Through him, a person who has reached the end can find himself again at the beginning of things.[33]

In another version, this passage reads:

> In this person, a great spiritual researcher, "a life dedicated completely to the service of truth," lives before us as a model and lives for us. Before him, even the most independent person may reflect again and change; before him, in any case, one has done this who wanted to live according to the Word—*Vitam impendere vero* [his life dedicated to the truth].[34]
>
> ....

And the human being, who stood firmly
and seemed at the end of all knowing,
suddenly sees a world
turn incredibly upward.

Und der Mensch, der sich gestellt

schien an allen Wissens Ende,
sieht auf einmal eine Welt
unerhörter Aufwärtswende.[35]
[See the addendum concerning this poem.]

In his April 6, 1909, letter to Rudolf Steiner, in which he asked to be allowed to participate in a private lecture course, Christian Morgenstern expressed (two months after hearing his first anthroposophical lecture) the fact that he lived very much in seclusion, "for whom only your word and the subject matters."[36] Morgenstern was not a member of the German Section of the Theosophical Society, and thus he did not have the right to hear the Düsseldorf lecture course, *The Spiritual Hierarchies and the Physical World.* He sent several unpublished sonnets with his letter to Rudolf Steiner—who knew his published poetic work and valued it—and Rudolf Steiner gladly authorized and permitted him to attend the lectures in Düsseldorf. The course remained immeasurably significant to Morgenstern throughout his life. "Your word and the subject"—"*You pure spirit, / from your strong hands / I received anew my meaning of life.*"[37]

For Christian Morgenstern, it was not about the "German Section of the Theosophical Society" and its (somewhat obscure) lodges, customs, and practices, but rather about the essence of Anthroposophy—as well as the "pure spirit" of the one who brought it into the earthly and cultural world, the "first spiritual-scientific scholar and European writer" of "the whole present culture," as he wrote in 1913, four years after the lecture course in Düsseldorf. Morgenstern was spiritual enough to recognize that the being of Rudolf

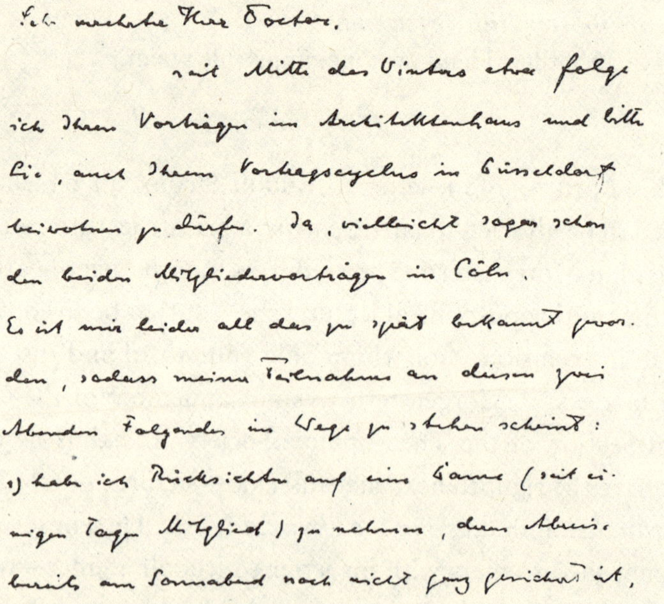

Sehr verehrter Herr Doktor,

seit Mitte des Winters etwa folge ich Ihren Vorträgen im Architektenhaus und bitte Sie, auch Ihrem Vortragscyclus in Düsseldorf beiwohnen zu dürfen. Ja, vielleicht sogar schon den beiden Mitgliedervorträgen in Cöln.

Es ist mir leider all das zu spät bekannt worden, sodass meiner Teilnahme an diesen zwei Abenden Folgendes im Wege zu stehen scheint:

1) habe ich Rücksichten auf eine Dame (seit einigen Tagen Mitglied) zu nehmen, deren Abreise bereits am Sonnabend noch nicht ganz gesichert ist,

2) bin ich noch nicht Mitglied (wiewohl bereit es zu werden, wenn sich die nötigen Bürgen so rasch finden) und 3) möchte ich (sowohl wie sie) nichts vorwegnehmen.

Ich brauche diesen letzten Punkten Ihnen gegenüber nichts hinzuzufügen, als höchstens dies, dass ich ein sehr zurückgezogen lebender Mensch bin, dem lediglich Ihr Wort und die Sache am Herzen liegen.

Wie stark ich mich Ihnen selbst, verehrter Herr Dr.,

Letter from Christian Morgenstern to Rudolf Steiner
April 6, 1909

verbunden fühle, dafür mag Ihnen das beige-
legte Sonettenpaar aus meinem jüngsten noch
ungedruckten Buche wie ein froher dankbarer
Ostergruss sein.

Ihr

Ihnen aufrichtig ergebener

Christian Morgenstern.

z. Z. Berlin W. 6. IV. 09.
Derfflingerstr. 14 III.

Nachschrift. Um Ihnen Zeitverlust und mir Un-
gewissheit zu ersparen, erlaube ich mir Ihnen
vorzuschlagen, mir mit beigefügtem Porto –
bis spätestens Freitag mittag einen telegra-
phischen Permiss für Düsseldorf auszustellen
(und falls es Ihnen möglich und richtig erscheint
allenfalls auch einen für Cöln.) Sollten Sie mei-
ne Zeilen aber zu spät erreichen, so erbitte ich diese
Antwort nach Hotel Terminus, Cöln.

Steiner and the spirit of Anthroposophy stood in deep relationship with each other without being identical.

Rudolf Steiner "founded," according to Christian Morgenstern, "Spiritual Science of the human being as a cosmic being—Anthroposophy." At least from an earthly perspective, he was its creator, and further, it's messenger or witness. He represented Anthroposophy and represented it in such a way that one could experience from his words and from his being what it was about spiritually and morally, even when one could not yet understand initially or have an overview of all the details of the teaching. About a deeply moving lecture course in Budapest that Rudolf Steiner held in the summer of 1909, "*Theosophie und Okkultismus des Rosenkreuzers*" [Theosophy and Occultism of the Rosicrucians, CW 109], Morgenstern wrote to his future wife, "I, at least, need the personal living guarantee of Steiner himself with these immense cosmic images."[38]

Christian Morgenstern did not distrust any of the contents presented; indeed, it resounded deeply in his heart. Yet for him, Rudolf Steiner was the "living guarantor" of "Spiritual Science of the human as a cosmic being," who is indispensable as such. From his "pure spirit," Christian Morgenstern received not only a fundamental deepening of his life and his understanding of life—being himself placed again "at the beginning of things"—he also experienced in the spiritual leader, above and beyond the content of the teaching, the meaning of *Spirit recalling, Spirit awareness,* and *Spirit beholding,* and how it virtually took place before his eyes. At the same time, he experienced Rudolf Steiner the fighter. Steiner stood with all his strength against obstacles to a new beginning, indeed the true turning point of civilization. He gave his all for it and walked a sorrowful path of sacrifice, though with "strong hands" and incomparable energy. "Great philosophical moment during the lecture of August 27, 1913: I saw for a moment the human being (Steiner) as pure, conscious will, maintaining himself only through an immense divine will to move forward in life."[39] A decade later, at the end of September 1923, Rudolf Steiner would say:

> Have trust in the thoughts of the spirit if you can receive them at all, so that you know you have received a spiritual impulse. You surrender yourself to it and make yourself an instrument for its execution. First failure—never mind! Second failure—never mind! If there are a hundred failures, they are of no consequence, since no failure is ever a decisive factor in judging the truth of a spiritual impulse that has been understood and grasped inwardly. Only then do we have trust, proper trust, in a spiritual impulse that we have grasped at a certain point in time, when we can say to ourselves: I have failed a hundred times, but that proves to me at most that the conditions for realizing that impulse are not given to me in this incarnation. However, I see through its own character that this impulse is correct. Even if it takes a hundred incarnations before the powers to realize this impulse arise for me, nothing can convince me of the efficacy or impotence of a spiritual impulse other than its own nature.
>
> When you imagine this thought developed in the human mind and heart [*Gemüt*] as a great trust or confidence in something spiritual, when you think that human beings can hold firmly to what they have seen as spiritually victorious—as something not to be relinquished despite all outer opposition—then you will have an idea of what the Michael power, or Michael being, wants from the human being; only then will you have a concept of

> great trust in the spirit. You can set aside some spiritual impulse—even set it aside for your whole incarnation—but once you understand it you may never waver from giving it great care and attention within yourself. Only then can you save it for future incarnations. Once trust in the spirit has established a frame of mind in this way and you come to experience this spiritual impulse as concretely as the ground beneath your feet—which we know we need to stand—then you have in your *Gemüt* a feeling of what Michael really wants of us.[40]

In a letter to Margareta Gosebruch von Liechtenstern in October 1908, three months before he met Rudolf Steiner and Anthroposophy, Christian Morgenstern had written, "As a result, precisely *that* shall be the ideal of my life—courage and determination to the last in all that is spiritual."[41]

~

In this connection, immediately following his first encounter with Rudolf Steiner on January 28, 1909, Christian Morgenstern was already clear that the maturity of soul forces one could experience in him and that reach the point of "pure, conscious willing" also had to become his own goal of development and his inner path. Rudolf Steiner was the teacher, witness, and "guarantor" of Anthroposophy not only on the level of its content, but just as clearly so in the realm of its "form"—the development of its form in the individual human being. The essence of Anthroposophy is that its own being consists of the being of the human, and that is the essence of its effectiveness—that individuals receive in Anthroposophy what they themselves are and must place it before their own being, because human beings must practice self-knowledge.

At the beginning of 1909, Morgenstern wrote decisively,

> *To learn to concentrate evermore consciously. To overcome everything that flutters and flickers within me. To hang a stone to anchor every good thought and every good feeling. Connected with that: become settled; subdue one's haste; control one's pace.*[42]

Consequently, he not only practiced the so-called subsidiary exercises on the path of the esoteric schooling, but also formulated them in poetic form.

I

Amid what, in our thinking,
mostly without our help, flows through us,
he decided, having collected himself, to sink
into an unmediated, freely chosen
thought, and let it sink firmly into him;
and so, thus cultivated rigorously,
the forces of his capacity to think
    grew strong as steel in him.

II

Freed from thinking's oscillation,
he also began to free his will
that far too long had borne the same yoke—
methodically interrupting and correcting
the necessities of daily duties and actions
during certain periods by his own action—
forces streamed from his heart to his head.

III

As long as we cannot with calm composure
bear joy and suffering alike,
we will not understand the world.

Without love and without hate we must ask
pain and passion for their meaning.
Only so will the senses' deception pale to appearance,
only then can God speak His Word to us.

IV

Before a putrid, dead, decaying dog
the Master Jesus slowed His step,
unlike His fleeing circle of distraught disciples.
Then, among them, indignantly the whisper arose:
What, at the sight of a corpse,
was to retch a sickness of soul?
Then, with shame, they heard his response:
He was in awe at the animal's white teeth.

V

Spare me your fairytale rubbish!
The Tower of Pisa stands upright—since yesterday!
In my worldview, there is no room for miracles.
Truly, you should be ashamed of your worldview.
Surely you should not feed superstition,
but rather, undoubtedly acknowledge grace,
which declares war on your weakness of faith.

VI

Creature no longer, ruler of thoughts,
Lord of the will, no longer its servant,
Measure and Master of surging feeling,
too deep to get sick from denial,
too free for stubbornness to live in him or her;
in this way, one bonds with the realm of spirits;
thus, one finds the path to the Throne of Thrones.

I

Inmitten dessen, was als unser Denken
zumeist ohn unser Zutun uns durchflüchtet,
beschloß er, sich gesammelt zu versenken
In einen unvermittelt frei gewählten
Gedanken und ihn fest sich einzusenken:
dass sich ihm, also streng gezüchtet,
Die Kräfte reinen Denkvermögens stählten.

II

Wie so des Denkens Schwingen sich befreiten,
begann er auch sein Wollen zu entbannen,
das allzulang ins gleiche Joch geschirrte:
indem es planvoll die Notwendigkeiten
des Tagwerkhandelns auf gewisse Spannen
durch eigenhandeln unterbrach und irrte—
daß Ströme Kraft von Herz zu Haupt ihm rannen.

III

So lange wir nicht ruhevoll-gelassen
vermögen Glück und Unglück zu ertragen,
so lange werden wir die Welt nicht fassen.
Wir müssen ohne Lieben, ohne Hassen
so Leid wie Lust nach ihrem Sinne fragen.
Nur so wird Sinnentrug zu Schein verblassen,
nur dann vermag uns Gott Sein Wort zu sagen.

IV

Vor einem widerlich verwesten Hunde
beschränkt der Meister Jesus seine Schritte,
ungleich der Flücht verstörter Jüngerrunde.
Was soll's? so raunt's empört aus deren Mitte:
wär, sich vor Aas zu eleln, kranke Laune?

Da hören sie, beschämt, auf ihre Bitte,
Daß er des Tieres weiß Gebiß bestaune.

V

Verschone mich mit deinem Märchenplunder!
Der Turm von Pisa sei seit gestern—gerade?
In meinem Weltbild ist kein Raum für Wunder.
Fürwahr, so ist es um dein Weltbild schade.
Du sollst gewiß nicht Aberglauben nähren,
doch ebenso gewißlich sonder Gnade
der—Glaubens-Ohnmacht in dir—Krieg erklären.

VI

Geschöpf nicht mehr, Gebieter der Gedanken,
des Willens Herr, nicht mehr in Willens Frone,
der flutenden Empfindung Maß und Meister,
Zu tief, um an Verneinung zu erkranken,
zu frei, als dass Verstocktheit in ihm wohne:
So bindet sich ein Mensch ans Reich der Geister:
So findet er den Pfad zum Thron der Throne.[43]

Christian Morgenstern experienced Rudolf Steiner as the spiritual teacher of individual human beings and world culture in general, and thus Morgenstern saw Steiner as the teacher and heart of a spiritual community through his public lectures—for example, in the Berlin Architect House, as well as in his books. Beyond this, beginning with his participation in the internal course in Düsseldorf on the spiritual hierarchies, . As foreign as some things were in the beginning for Morgenstern, he was soon just as clear that Rudolf Steiner placed trust in the spiritual community formed around and for the being *Anthroposophia,* whom he brought into the midst of the community. Anthroposophy was for him not just a significant teaching and a methodical path of knowledge; it also had an existence, or being, of its own. In that existence, however, Anthroposophy seemed to need human beings to join together to be present on Earth *and* to be able to be effective. Rudolf Steiner did not want or need an organizational form—neither for himself nor for anthroposophic Spiritual Science; however, he did indeed need a community of knowledge and action made up of determined individuals who bear within themselves a binding relationship to and responsibility for Anthroposophy.

In autumn 1919, years after Morgenstern's death, Rudolf Steiner would say in a Berlin lecture, "Those who unite in the community we call 'the movement of anthroposophically oriented Spiritual Science' should feel they form a core from which the force for a new social form radiates. What comes from other sides for social reform can be very useful, but it needs to be worked on. True social reform comes only through spiritual impulses."[44]

Since his youth, Christian Morgenstern had consciously experienced and painfully suffered through the drama of materialism and its destructive consequences in science, art, religion, and social life. It became clear to him early on that "social reformation" could certainly not be achieved with socialistic (or other) party programs, but required fresh thinking—especially in regard to the human being—presupposing also new values and goals based on a true spiritual life. In Anthroposophy, Morgenstern found not only this spiritual life, but at the same time (coming from Rudolf Steiner) an effort to form a spiritual work community of people for the future, from which "the force for social reform" could truly radiate in connection with the necessary courage and trust.

> If you have the ability to receive them at all, have trust in the thoughts of the spirit, so that you know you have received a spiritual impulse. Surrender yourself to it and make yourself an instrument for its execution. First failure—never mind! Second failure—never mind! When there are a hundred failures, they are of no consequence, for no failure is ever decisive in judging the truth of a spiritual impulse that has been understood and grasped inwardly. Only then do we have trust, proper trust, in a spiritual impulse...

Christian Morgenstern's friend Michael Bauer wrote about Rudolf Steiner, "He saw ever more clearly human beings at a developmental point, where only their *will* could bring about a favorable turn. He saw also that knowledge depends on that will. In the end, his work became a unique effort to encourage human beings."[45]

For the spiritual community it was decisively significant that Anthroposophy created a "social foundation" within it. It was a social foundation "in which human beings can know the human being," as Rudolf Steiner said in the Berlin Architect House on March 4, 1909, in Christian Morgenstern's presence. *"Spiritual Science is the basis of life, and love is the flower and fruit of such a life stimulated by Spiritual Science."*[46]

Christian Morgenstern experienced in Rudolf Steiner especially the fact that it is actually possible to make one's "capacity to love into a power of knowledge."[47] He saw that human love is not just the goal, but that it is also an actual result of studying Anthroposophy and its path of schooling—or could be—and that love is, in turn, beneficial for knowledge in a dialectical way. Rudolf Steiner showed not only theoretically but also quite concretely that penetrating real-world, human connections is a matter of "realizing selflessness" or the devotion of a fully conscious and active "I" to the content and beings. It is devotion that carries a heightened capacity to love or is even identical with it. With this love and warmth—"radiant warmth," according to Friedrich Hiebel—Rudolf Steiner also worked within the Anthroposophical Society, for which he seemed willing to give his all. This Society was to become the effective bearer and cultural ferment of a new age and new understanding of the human being.

> Human love that instructs us about human worth will be kindled in us through anthroposophical spiritual-scientific insights that strive to enter the suprasensory, allowing us to feel the dignity of being human. Knowledge of human worth, feeling for human dignity, and willing in human love—these are the most beautiful fruits of life instilled in human beings through experiencing the results of Spiritual Science."[48]

At the same time, shortly after his first acquaintance with Rudolf Steiner's lectures and writings, it was substantially significant for Christian Morgenstern that the acknowledgment of reincarnation is also a part of the anthroposophical consideration and view of the human being. Morgenstern had already adopted this view years before any contact with Anthroposophy. Now, through anthroposophic Spiritual Science, he encountered not only a view of the human being that unfolded the idea of reincarnation to the last detail, but also, in a certain sense, placed it as a central social or community foundation. "The way and manner through which people become convinced of reincarnation and karma, as well as how they find the possibility of bringing the thought of reincarnation into ordinary life, will change this modern life substantially, from now and into the future. It will create entirely new forms of living and a completely new way of coming together as human beings."[49] Rudolf Steiner formulated this not only as a general statement but, in view of the Anthroposophical Society, also said:

> May anthroposophists feel consciously how they collaborate to bring forth a new culture. This sense, or feeling, of the immense significance of reincarnation and karma for life—this would be something that could hold a group of people together today, despite the outer circumstances of those people. Those who are held together by this view can find their way to one another only through Anthroposophy.[50]

In precisely this way, after overcoming the first social hurdles, Christian Morgenstern grasped and accepted the formation of anthroposophical community, which he understood to be the beginning of a future society.

> Those who regard individuals as wanderers who always return will cease working against them. One imagines going side-by-side with them and recognizing the senselessness of any enmity between oneself and others. Should others still wish to feel enmity, one will no longer feel that they are an enemy. For such individual, when looking at the others *sub specie aeterni* [from the perspective of eternity], the two nearly coincide with each other. Should the others still hate them, they will want nothing but to help those others, to be useful, to serve...[51]

For more than five years after January 1909, Christian Morgenstern followed Rudolf Steiner's support for the development of this anthroposophical community. This included the four Mystery Dramas (1910–1913), which occurred during Morgenstern's time in the anthroposophical movement. The Mystery Dramas have to do with the destinies in an esoteric (reincarnation) community, the paths and wrong paths of the individuals involved and their pursuit of a higher goal. Morgenstern, who had a comprehensive understanding of the dramatic arts, and who had (like Rudolf Steiner) dedicated years of his life to modern theatrical art and its development, was one of the most knowledgeable and insightful witnesses of the dramas and their intentions in connection with the anthroposophical community.

Afterward, he followed with great attentiveness the way the Mystery Drama performances gave rise to the intention in the Anthroposophical Society for a future "Johannes Building." From the very beginning, Christian Morgenstern felt connected to the Johannes Building project as a center for renewed sciences, arts, and religion in the form of the "Independent School for Spiritual Science" with a civilizational purpose. Indeed, it corresponded to his own deepest wish of heart and destiny. He read Rudolf Steiner's statements in an early, October 1911 circular from the Johannes Building Association:

> The thought of a *School for Spiritual Science is the certain consequence that must be drawn from the distribution of spiritual knowledge* acknowledged in our time. When we let the coworkers among us pass before our mind's eye, it is absolutely possible today to name experienced teachers in almost every field who, when asked, gladly accept a teaching post. With that, Spiritual Science would first be

> able to do justice to the task that was given to it from the beginning: to fructify all areas of life. From the academies, the School for Spiritual Science will take knowledge that is capable of evolving—whereas its official representatives today allow it to rigidify into materialism—and lead it upward to knowledge of the spirit and take it into the temple, where its union with art and religion makes a living mystery possible.[52]

Nine years earlier, in 1902, Christian Morgenstern noted in his "Roman Diary":

> One yearns for a great cult in common, similar to those of antiquity, for only such a cultus can give an art the highest goals.... What people call "art" today prepares this. As yet, the hand or spirit that unites is lacking. Increasingly, it is getting through to our people, but still does not reach everyone. Only when it does will we have a culture—when this folk, unable to remain standing on the path of merely private art, rises upward to seek a higher expression of its passion for the elevation of life. Once it has begun, there will be ventured—in addition to the hundreds of thousands of excellent functional, practical buildings and decorative buildings—the first building that wishes to express its new *soul*. Then this ideal building may be called the *beginning of our culture*. The greatest of our painters and sculptors will have their home in it; the poets and musicians of great style will find in it their house. Until then, we are all wanderers.[53]

During autumn 1912, a year after the first circular from the Johannes Building Association, Christian Morgenstern first expressed in a letter to his wife his hope that Rudolf Steiner, after separating from the Theosophical Society, would come and bring the anthroposophical movement to the area around Basel, Switzerland ("and work further

Christian Morgenstern's entry ticket to the premier of "The Souls' Awakening" Rudolf Steiner's fourth mystery drama (Munich, August 1913)

from here"[54]). A few days later, Rudolf Steiner was on Dornach Hill for the first time and received an offer of that hill for the Johannes Building. For health reasons, Christian Morgenstern was unable to take part in laying the Foundation Stone of the building in September 1913; nor could his friend Michael Bauer, who wrote to him "that we knowingly experience, at least in thought, the moment when a mystery center once again blesses the Earth after two thousand years of being deprived. This surely belongs to the most important things in our life. Now, when we are born once again, we will hope to find the way to such centers with more certainty."[55]

A poem by Christian Morgenstern reads:

Softly on delicate feet it draws near,
before sleep, like a gentle breeze:
Hear, o soul, my counsel,
may good luck and comfort smile upon you—

Those bound to you in love,
will always remain around you,
will loyally describe small
and great circles with you.

And they will rely on you,
unrelated, as you to them—
and, awakened to seeing,
you vie with them in serving!

Leis auf zarten Füßen naht es,
vor dem Schlafen wie ein Fächeln:
Horch, o Seele, meines Rates,
laß dir Glück und Tröstung lächeln—:

Die in Liebe dir verbunden,
werden immer um dich bleiben,

werden klein und große Runden
treugesellt mit dir beschreiben.

Und sie werden an dir bauen,
unverwandt, wie du an ihnen,—
und, erwacht zu einem Schauen,
werdet ihr wetteifernd dienen![56]

Morgenstern's lines are connected with the development of the human being in a karmic community: individual development with the help of the others. They spoke of a *building* on the being of the human being; it was also a matter of such a "building" in Dornach. An Independent School for Spiritual Science was to be "built" as a place where future mysteries would be possible. In addition, the "building" had to be the work of a spiritually awakened community—"awake to beholding..."

≈

Rudolf Steiner's efforts all "served" the intention of the "building," and, insofar as possible and his strength allowed, Christian Morgenstern wanted from the beginning to help him with it. In late spring 1909, he decided to travel to Budapest for the Congress of the Theosophical Society, despite severe illness and the exhausting heat, intending to lend his assistance. *"[Rudolf Steiner] is a leader of humanity, and it means something to meet one so seldom in life and, as a mature human being, to be allowed freely and lovingly to help to a certain extent."*[57] If Alfred Guttmann, the letter's recipient, had asked Christian Morgenstern at the time how he could be "helpful" to Rudolf Steiner in Budapest, Morgenstern would have been at a loss to give a concrete answer. In the depths of

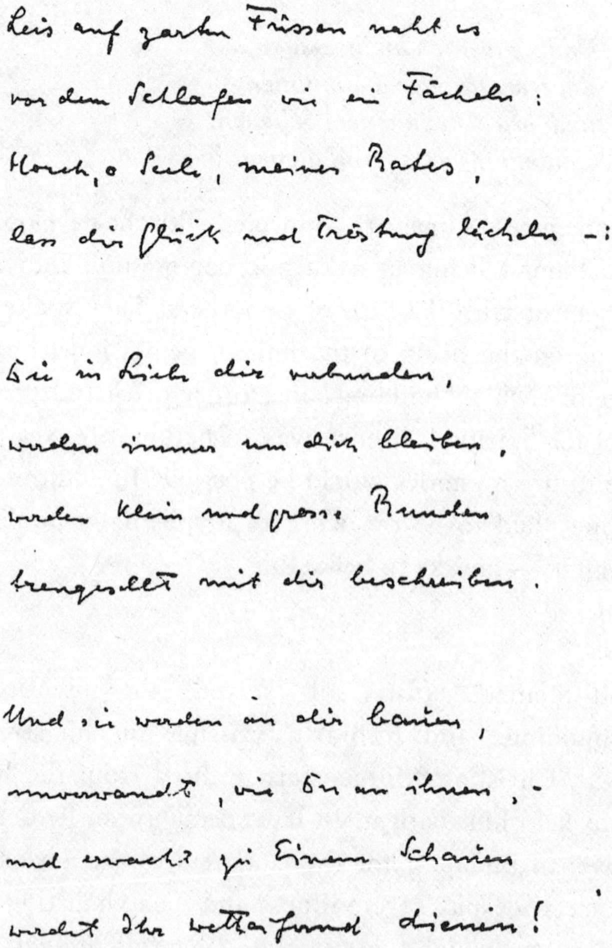

Leis auf zarten Füssen naht es
vor dem Schlafen wie ein Fächeln:
Horch, o Seele, meines Rates,
lass dir Glück und Tröstung lächeln –:

Die in Liebe dir verbunden,
werden immer um dich bleiben,
werden klein und grosse Runden
treugesellt mit dir beschreiben.

Und sie werden an dir bauen,
unverwandt, wie du an ihnen, –
und erwacht zu Einem Schauen
werdet Ihr Weltengrund dienen!

Christian Morgenstern's handwriting (August 20, 1909)

his being, however, he seemed to know about the struggle taking place, at the heart of which was Rudolf Steiner's work in the Theosophical Society. This involved arguments centered essentially on spiritual Rosicrucianism and Christology, and therefore on the core of Anthroposophy itself. There is much to suggest that he felt how essential his mere presence in the lecture hall—his spiritual presence—would be for Rudolf Steiner.

Christian Morgenstern had special destiny tasks and a great sensibility and selflessness. Who besides him, with such goals and absolutely no financial means, would be willing and able to set out on a sixteen-hour train trip (third class) from Berlin to Budapest, while being plagued by flares of fever and living at the edge of his physical forces? Christian Morgenstern wrote[58] that the "meaning of life consists of the infinitely enlivened and intensified communion of beings," or a "conversation of the highest kind of give-and-take." He always attempted to maintain this viewpoint in his relationship to Rudolf Steiner. Moreover, Christian Morgenstern was an exception in this way within the anthroposophical movement.

Rudolf Steiner valued Christian Morgenstern's presence in his Christology courses, at no cost, of course—that is, not at the cost of Morgenstern's health or existence on Earth. ("I could see then how the severe breakdown of his health and his body was approaching."[59]) The progressing tuberculosis that afflicted Morgenstern threatened his life, and he required protection, rest, and a retreat instead of an overcrowded and overheated lecture hall. Both directly and through Margareta Gosebruch von Liechtenstern,

Rudolf Steiner repeatedly let Christian Morgenstern know, throughout the summer and fall of 1909, that in view of his physical condition Morgenstern urgently needed to take a break. Following a conversation with Steiner on September 27, 1909, in Basel, Margareta wrote to her fiancé:

> All of this must now be transferred into your productivity and must fructify it. This is essential now, not that something new should come in addition. In any case, you have received "so much of the esoteric" through your exercises and so on that he could no longer give you anything further anyway.[60]

At the time, Christian Morgenstern had already become a member of Rudolf Steiner's Esoteric School and—in addition to having attended the large courses in Düsseldorf, Christiania (Oslo), Budapest, Kassel, and Munich, as well as single lectures in Berlin, Cologne, and Koblenz—had also received personal meditation instructions from him ("your exercises"). For Rudolf Steiner, it was important that Christian Morgenstern should protect himself, and that he continue resolutely with his own literary life task.

Twelve years later, in a conversation with the Swiss writer Albert Steffen and the English sculptor Edith Maryon at the beginning of January 1922, Rudolf Steiner asserted, "*Germany was in danger of losing the spirit that lives in the German language and [in danger], with its way of thinking dissolving into that of the folk dialect, whereas the German word has an absolutely cosmopolitan disposition to become the spirit messenger and bearer of esotericism.*"[61]

On the basis of this background, Rudolf Steiner was more than grateful for Christian Morgenstern's life work and highly valued the fact that Morgenstern united himself so intensively with Anthroposophy. According to Steiner, Anthroposophy not only has "tasks of formal knowledge," but also has to accomplish "creative historic tasks," among which is the development and training of human speech, which has essential significance for future evolution.[62] From the beginning, Rudolf Steiner attached great importance to language and the work of the Logos—the "Christ impulse" in language—in his anthroposophical work. He also brought Anthroposophy itself into connection with "finding the Word that has been lost."[63]

From year to year, Christian Morgenstern's literary work became more and more permeated with anthroposophic Spiritual Science. It remained independent and founded in itself; and yet in its way, it gave witness to what occurred as a spiritual beginning of the twentieth century and was closely connected with Rudolf Steiner. In the winter of 1912, Morgenstern wrote the following lines in Arosa:

For Dr. Rudolf Steiner

Just as a person, on a cloudy day, forgets the Sun—
while it, however, rays and shines continuously—
so, too, one may forget your Sun on a cloudy day,
in order, again and ever again,
shaken, yes, struck blind, to feel,
how inexhaustibly on and on and on
your Sun-Spirit
blazes out to us dark wanderers.

Für Dr. Rudolf Steiner

So wie ein Mensch, am trüben Tag, der Sonne vergißt,—
sie aber strahlt und leuchtet unaufhörlich,—
so mag man Dein an trübem Tag vergessen,
um wiederum und immer wiederum
erschüttert, ja geblendet zu empfinden,
wie unerschöpflich fort und fort und fort
Dein Sonnengeist
uns dunklen Wandrern strahlt.[64]

Marie Steiner-von Sivers described one of the final meetings between Christian Morgenstern and Rudolf Steiner on the morning of November 24, 1913, in Stuttgart, following two of Rudolf Steiner's Christological lectures from *The Fifth Gospel* (Nov. 22 and 23) and a recitation of Morgenstern's poetry. Her brief and thoroughly succinct formulations show the mystery of the life meeting of Morgenstern and Steiner, in the harmony of life tasks or in a "conversation of the highest kind of mutual give-and-take."

> That day Christian Morgenstern appeared as if relieved of his suffering and happy. Anyone who experienced his smiling face at that time will never forget it. That complete understanding of each other and passing over into one another of two great spirits created an atmosphere, perceptible to everyone, that had an uplifting power and radiated hope for the future.[65]

Christian Morgenstern, 1913

2

"A Human Star"

Evidence of Anthroposophy in the Realm of the Dead and the Unborn

Rudolf Steiner spoke repeatedly about his spiritual friend at memorial events and in Branch lectures during the first year after Christian Morgenstern's death (until Holy Saturday 1915). He spoke of the earthly life just behind him and in particular about his continuing significance. He began within a few days after the cremation in Basel, on Good Friday, April 10, 1914, before the beginning of his scheduled lecture in Vienna. He said, *"Allow me, before the lecture begins, to let the solemn ceremony reverberate somewhat, which some of us attended a few days ago near our building in Basel."*[66] Christian Morgenstern had certainly wanted to travel to Vienna to attend the lecture course on life after death (*The Inner Nature of Man,* CW 153). ("I had so hoped to be able to come to Vienna."[67]). In the end, it was no longer possible. Rudolf Steiner, however, included the friend in every respect and brought to expression for the members of the Anthroposophical Society the degree of "heartfelt gratitude and heartfelt love" with which he followed Morgenstern's path in Anthroposophy—Christian Morgenstern whose "delicate, loving soul" was in a position to live "so wonderfully" in "solitary spiritual heights."

> We saw how much he suffered, as well as how high he soared in his poetry, which revealed so wonderfully his glorious soul. Indeed, we can consider it our anthroposophical movement's great good fortune to have had Christian Morgenstern in our midst these past years. What we are studying, what we want to immerse ourselves in regarding the spiritual worlds—that is what we could hear resounding so beautifully and grandly in Christian Morgenstern's poetry. He created our spiritual studies and endeavors in his poems. Moreover, he—who became so thoroughly united with our movement that his suffering and highest poetic flight became one with the innermost goals of our anthroposophical life—ennobled our movement. Indeed, Christian Morgenstern belonged wholeheartedly to us; he was one of us with everything in him that he could lift, as well as with everything he experienced in recent years in his ailing body, which presented him with so many obstacles. He was one of us with all his suffering, because he belonged to us with all his feelings.
>
> One has to admire the way he accepted his suffering and the obstacles he encountered in the physical-sensory realm; when living in our ideas, views, and experiences, he felt reflected within himself what was revealed to us poetically![68]

Christian Morgenstern created an "artistic reincarnation of Anthroposophy" through his being, his inner effort, and his poetic works—"deep, intimate, and heartfelt community existed between us." Rudolf Steiner said further:

> Those who were close to him felt how wonderful it was to know that, even when he sought rest or improved

> health in the Swiss mountains and was far away from us, he remained spiritually united with us. I felt uplifted and warmed to know that here or there, while I was in one or another city, he was speaking about spiritual things. It warms my heart to know that he was dwelling there in the Swiss mountains, living poetically on the same spiritual heights as I was, walking with me on my journey through the lands of the soul.[69]

> During those times, we could think that, while we were working here to convey to human souls what had been entrusted to us to share, there was someone living up there in the Swiss Alps who never ceased in his efforts to wed his poetic power to what our spiritual movement had to reveal. We could bask in the knowledge that up in the mountains there was someone in whom lived what we are trying to realize and experience firsthand in our Spiritual Science. It was blossoming in him in a unique and individual way, born anew from his poetic powers.[70]

Never before had Rudolf Steiner spoken in this way about a spiritual student—an actual coworker—in the anthroposophical movement. His researches and spiritual experiences were carried out intensively and experienced with him by Morgenstern (*"passing through soul land with me"*) in a quite concrete (and at the same time "quite intimate") "spiritual community." In his poetry, according to Rudolf Steiner, Morgenstern recreated the anthroposophical study and work and its results. He lived "poetically" in anthroposophical ideas and "reflected... what is revealed to us" in the sense of a "new birth" through poetic power.

Although Rudolf Steiner did not take himself into account to a great extent, it was recognizable even in his addresses in Stuttgart and Leipzig (November and December 1913), that the process described had to do with him, too. This was not, however, the main emphasis of his presentation, but rather Morgenstern's work and life accomplishments—his high poetic and uplifting dynamic, "the wonderful revelations of a marvelous human soul." In Vienna, he said of Morgenstern's special spirituality, the basis of his unique poetry:

> Christian Morgenstern carried within himself what he had taken from the heredity bequeathed to him by his ancestors, who were painters. He had the closest inner kinship with nature, especially with the spirit of nature. He was familiar with the most delicate and secret activities of nature; and what nature spoke to his soul he allowed to reverberate and linger. So nature bore witness to him of the elemental beings and spoke to him with their voices, the voices of the elemental spirits that surge and waft through nature. Because of everything his deep soul could discover about nature through a kindred, intimate experience of it, Christian Morgenstern was able to rise to feelings and sentiments toward the universe that turn art into a hymn. In such a hymn, the mysteries of creation resound, and art ultimately becomes prayer. Few poets have been able to transform the tone of poetry into that of prayer as Christian Morgenstern did. He understood and could express the poetic, artistic and anthroposophical prayer to the spirit that suffuses and rules nature."[71]

On another occasion, Rudolf Steiner explained regarding the anthroposophical movement, "*I would like to say that it belongs to the very greatest evidence of the inner kernel of truth and ideal of truth that we are seeking with our soul that, from the spiritual ground that we attempt to achieve, we see poetry spring forth from such depths of heart.*"[72]

Rudolf Steiner not only valued Christian Morgenstern's poems, but he was also able to read their essence; in other words, he could penetrate to their inner kernel. At the end of

1913 in Leipzig, he emphasized (in Morgenstern's presence) that the mood he experienced in connection to the poetic cycle *We Have Found a Path* was, for him, "*something blissful regarding the inner power of the soul that leads into the spirit realm.*"[73]

Without a doubt, Rudolf Steiner experienced the convergence of his own path of knowledge with the culminating work of a "poet of the spirit," whose final poems were inspired "directly from the spiritual life and had a special '*aura*.'" Rudolf Steiner had first spoken briefly about this "aura" in Leipzig, so as to go more into detail now, following Morgenstern's death: "That aura will stream forth from many sounds in the poems, which you will hear shortly [in the recitation]. They are such that it's as though they had truly been spoken already from the spirit land by a soul for whom existence in the spirit land is fully conscious."[74] "We can feel the anthroposophical life and orientation of the mind stream directly from them as an aura. In other words, by reading his poems we experience something not in the words but *between* the words; not in the lines but *between* the lines; this is their unmediated auric life."[75]

Indeed, according to Rudolf Steiner, the *Christ impulse* lives as the heart of Anthroposophy in Morgenstern's poetry, which reached its peak in his final years of life. ("This meant spiritual-scientifically that the Christ impulse lives beautifully in these poems."[76]) "They are connected with truly *Rosicrucian-Christian moods.*"[77]

Although Rudolf Steiner expressed himself on this in a restrained way, much importance was indicated with his words about Morgenstern's life work in the beginning of the twentieth century with regard to the spiritual-historical basis of the anthroposophical movement. In Munich on November 20, 1911, Rudolf Steiner emphasized, "The most powerful help for understanding the Christ impulse in our time proceeds from the spiritual stream connected with Christian Rosenkreutz."[78]

Christian Morgenstern had never intended to write poetry only for the members of the Anthroposophical Society, or even for its esoteric school, but always turned toward all humankind. According to Rudolf Steiner, Morgenstern's poems can and should speak to all people, reaching and moving them in their deepest being, and this precisely from the inner anthroposophical substance of the poems, their "Christ impulse." As Steiner himself was, Christian Morgenstern was also oriented in this toward what is universally human, and connected with the work and motives of the Rosicrucian stream, with faith in the acceptance of his poetry—which is inconspicuous on the surface—and faith in spiritualization with their help. He would gladly have published *We Have Found a Path* with "theosophical" annotations in the appendix,[79] and as early as 1911 he was planning an anthology of introductory texts of modern Spiritual Science. "I am occupying myself in the theosophical field with my plan for an anthology from theosophical works that will serve as a kind of introduction for those who are unacquainted [with Theosophy]."[80]

≈

In Vienna, as well as in later lectures, Rudolf Steiner repeatedly made it clear that the presence—indeed the active collaboration—of Christian Morgenstern must be counted among the most beneficial strokes of destiny for the anthroposophical movement. He not only pointed out

Image of the Rose Cross from the estate of Ita Wegman

how inwardly prepared Morgenstern was when he entered the movement at the beginning of 1909 through his training and deep "yearning" for the spiritual life ("as prepared as ever possible"), but he also stated that Christian Morgenstern absorbed Anthroposophy as such with corresponding intensity. Steiner described Morgenstern as an example of the "best anthroposophist,"[81] calling his way of living into spiritual-scientific content "rich with blessing." Morgenstern was able to transform anthroposophical ideas directly "into personal feelings," however, and then carry all the personal up into a "suprapersonal sphere." His relationship to Anthroposophy and its being and content bore a character of incomparable devotion and "deep warmth of feeling."

Rudolf Steiner knew many students of Anthroposophy in various countries quite well; among them were excellent minds that possessed remarkable intellectual and devotional capacities. Nonetheless, the number of those who actually knew how to unite both directions of activity in their souls (or had adequately developed it) was not very great. Clearly, however, very special conditions existed in Christian Morgenstern's individuality. Rudolf Steiner went into greater detail about this spiritual kernel of Morgenstern's special way of taking in Anthroposophy, especially in Scandinavia, a region where he said that "the best conditions" exist for understanding the present Christ revelations.[82] In Norrköping, Sweden, he spoke about the spiritual friend:

> While he was with us, he took our teaching about the Christ into his being. He absorbed this anthroposophical teaching and connected it with his soul until it truly became the spiritual heart's blood of his soul; he received it in such a way that, for him, it contained the substance of

> the Christ. The Christ-being flowed into him through that teaching. At the same time, the Christ, as he lives in our movement, passed into his soul.[83]

Rudolf Steiner's presentations in Norrköping in July 1914, shortly before the outbreak of World War I (condensed into a few sentences) were definitely significant in terms of Christian Morgenstern's association with Anthroposophy and the anthroposophical movement itself: "The Christ, as he lives in our movement..." Later, Rudolf Steiner spoke about the possibility and need for a "spiritual communion." Here, however, during the summer of 1914, the motif appeared for the first time in an extraordinarily striking way—and this as an example of an esoteric master student and a "model" of an "exemplary anthroposophist." According to Rudolf Steiner, Anthroposophy lived in Christian Morgenstern, in a Christ-imbued way, as "Christ-permeated Anthroposophy" in its true nature.

On the eve of Christian Morgenstern's forty-third birthday, four weeks after his cremation in Basel, Rudolf Steiner discussed the fact that Morgenstern's inner work was significant not just for Morgenstern himself. Looking back over Morgenstern's final years of life and his intense interactions with the Anthroposophical Society—in study and meditation, penetration of its ideas, the experience of soul transformation, and the creative art of poetry—Rudolf Steiner spoke of the process connected with it:

> It is a fact of the spiritual world that a series of imaginations was prepared in his body—a body that showed symptoms of illness. A series of imaginations, powerful imaginations, lived in those sick limbs, so to speak. He was filled completely with the content of the spiritual

> worlds, which lived in him in such a way that they worked on all the organs of which we are generally unaware—such as awareness of our brain and nervous system—or the organs we experience mostly on a subconscious level. His powerful imaginations lived in those organs, and the more they did so, the more outwardly ill those organs became. They prepared themselves, and now they face the soul of the deceased as a mighty tableau of the spiritual world. Now he is living in the images that were trapped in his sick organs, especially during his final years. They prepared themselves with such intensity that they now surround him as his spiritual world.[84]

In his highly concentrated, active, and selfless meditative experience of absorbing Anthroposophy, as Morgenstern became filled completely with the "content of the spiritual world," according to Rudolf Steiner powerful imaginations prepared themselves in a concentrated way in his soul body. They were freed during the first weeks after death and began to light up "in wondrous beauty" in the spiritual world *"so that they would be perceived in the spiritual world [from then on] as a wonderful work of art of the spirit world—a work of art created from the cosmos."*[85]

Rudolf Steiner spoke of a "complete image of the cosmic evolution,"[86] "the spiritual cosmic-All flowing together,"[87] or a "wonderful component" of the cosmos.[88] In fact, Christian Morgenstern entered the anthroposophical movement at the time when Steiner's development of a Christian (or "Christ-imbued") cosmology was approaching its culmination. Morgenstern intensively pursued the corresponding lectures and written presentations he had long sought—indeed, had yearned for intensively over a span of many years—and recreated them in his poetry in many ways.

The Earth is the center point of the cosmos.
For it the Sun and planets arose.
They placed themselves around it.

After they emerged from the Thrones,
awoke to first existence as Old Saturn,
as Warmth-all—so the prophets see them—

sank then into cosmic sleep and night,
to resurrect again as Old Sun,
as fire–air (now on, now off),

rejuvenated then again in spirit stream
and, watery now, out as Old Moon
pushing the Sun, to the bliss of both,

taken back again in the house of the gods
for the last time, from it more condensed
as Earth-globe, beginning structure, finally,

to go forth, divided and ordered
in Sun, Moon and Earth, completed,
the cosmos prepares it as home for the "I,"

the fatherland of the Logos, and the Love.

Die Erde ist der Mittelpunkt der Welt.
Für sie entstanden Sonne und Planeten.
Sie haben sich um sie herumgestellt.

Nachdem sie aus der Throne Schoß getreten,
als Ursaturn, zum ersten Sein erwacht,
als Wärme-All—so schaun sie die Propheten—,

versunken dann in Weltenschlaf und -nacht,
um wiederaufzustehn als Alte Sonne,
als Feuerluft (bald an- bald abgefacht),

verjüngt dann abermals im Geisterbronne
und, wäßrig jetzt, als Alter Mond heraus
die Sonne stoßend, ihr und sich zur Wonne;

zurückgenommen in der Götter Haus
zum letzten Male, um aus ihm verdichter
als Erdball endlich, anfänglichen Baus,

hervorzugehn, zerteilt drauf und gesichtet
in Sonne, Mond und Erde, letzter Hand,
wird sie die Welt, dem Ich als Heim gerichtet,

des Logos und der Liebe Vaterland.[89]

According to Rudolf Steiner, as Christian Morgenstern continued his anthroposophic and poetic work, lofty spiritual beings worked from the realm of the archangels in his soul body and imprinted into it—"into his poetically blessed anthroposophical thoughts and ideas,"[90]—the "wonderful content of the cosmos," which stood before Morgenstern's individuality as a "powerful tableau" after his death. "*That he now has as his world outside himself in the spirit*..."

Rudolf Steiner indicated that Christian Morgenstern was karmically prepared for this deed, but during the first year after the death of the spiritual friend Steiner did not yet want to go into detail about the karmic relationships connected with it. On various occasions, however, he pointed out not only that the cosmic existence of the "powerful tableau" continued to work on the tasks given to Morgenstern's individuality for the future, but also that he spoke in preliminary sketches about his significance in the land of the dead and the unborn. Christian Morgenstern, who received the "substance" of the Christ-being in and with Anthroposophy and entered the spiritual world after death with a "thoroughly spiritualized consciousness illumined by Spiritual Science," was received there in a special way. "Permeated with consciousness of the new Christ proclamation, he carried new thoughts of the Christ evolution and its connection with humanity's upward evolution through the portal of death and into the spiritual worlds."[91] "One can say, my dear friends, that the entry to the spiritual world of the soul as embodied in Christian Morgenstern was an event for those spiritual worlds that was, in a certain sense, epochal (if I may use a prosaic expression) in the spiritual worlds."[92]

In London, during the spring of 1913, eleven months before Morgenstern's death, Rudolf Steiner described for the first time what had occurred in the spiritual world at the peak of the natural-scientifically determined materialism of the nineteenth century, speaking of a "second crucifixion" of the Christ-being in the etheric.

> More and more people took the result of their materialistic ideas on Earth with them when they entered the spiritual world through the portal of death, so that, beginning in the sixteenth century, more and more seeds of earthly materialism were carried over.... The seeds of earthly materialism that had been increasingly carried over during the sixteenth century by souls crossing the portal of death brought about increasing darkness and built the "dark sphere of materialism." Christ took this black sphere into his being, in the sense of Manichaeism, to transform it.... [The black sphere] brought about "spiritual death by suffocation" in the angelic being, in which the Christ-being has manifested since the Mystery of Golgotha. This sacrifice of Christ in the nineteenth century is comparable to the sacrifice on the physical plane through the Mystery of Golgotha and can be described as the second crucifixion

> of Christ in the etheric. The spiritual death by suffocation, which eliminated consciousness of the angel being in the worlds directly behind ours, is a repetition of the Mystery of Golgotha.[93]

Also during that spring, on May 2, 1913, in London, Steiner spoke in detail in a lecture for the first time about Michael's activity and his significance for the near future.

> Michael can give us new spiritual light, which we may regard as a transformation of the light given through him at the time of the Mystery of Golgotha, and people today may stand in this light. If we can experience this, we can also grasp the full meaning of the new age emerging right now from our own. We can notice the dawning of a spiritual revelation, which will enter the life of human beings on Earth during the next two centuries. In fact, since humanity is freer than it was previously, through our own will we will be able to advance to the point of being able to receive this revelation.[94]

As of March 31, 1914, the individuality of Christian Morgenstern carried Christ-imbued Anthroposophy—along with "new thoughts about the evolution of Christ and its connection with the evolution of humanity"—into the world of the spirit, characterized by difficult strife over the future of human beings. His entry to the sphere of the dead was, according to Rudolf Steiner, an "event" for the spiritual world and, most important, for the souls of the dead who had incarnated during the nineteenth century, and who, through Earth-related and earthbound thinking, feeling, and willing, brought about not only a heavy burden for the Earth's etheric realm, but also led to their own inability to find the cosmic image and nature of the human being again after death. Among those nearly lost souls, as Rudolf Steiner presented unexpectedly on Palm Sunday 1915, were the extraordinary minds of German Idealism, up to the appearance of the individuality of Christian Morgenstern.

> Such excellent souls have never carried into the spiritual world through the portal of death quite so much of what the earthly intellect can achieve and has no significance for the spiritual worlds, and what is there explains the sensory world. Insofar as the sensory worlds originate in the spiritual, deep spiritual secrets reveal the sensory worlds. For the most brilliant spirits, the environment into which they entered after death was a realm where strange manifestations shone toward their spiritual senses and mental faculties. Turning their inner vision downward, they had to look inward to the Earth to become aware that they are anything at all. One could say aphoristically: We see a gathering of souls that have gone through the portal of death into the spirit land—souls who, to the greatest extent possible, have carried into the spiritual worlds the most outstanding cycles of the earthly existence.
>
> Christian Morgenstern's soul entered their circle, a soul equipped with the deepest inner impulse for the spiritual-scientific (that is, with direct spiritual speech) and striving to experience what was supraearthly for the senses and suprasensory in the earthly realm. This soul strove to experience what enlivens and motivates the earthly human being in the power of the soul—what makes that soul receptive in the most eminent sense for all that shines toward the soul in spirit land after it has passed through the portal of death. Like a bright star that rises with the life that should be appropriated on Earth for the spirit land, Christian Morgenstern's soul entered amid those whose vision for such stars had already become dulled.
>
> Many brilliant spirits of past centuries could be named (Fichte, Schelling, Hegel) who went up through the portal of death and said: We have examined and discovered

the secrets of the Earth with our earthly intellect, but we remained empty of any understanding for what surrounds us now; it has remained empty, and empty was the answer to the great meaningful question of what the human being *is*, the living human being, in spirit land. The spirit embodied in Christian Morgenstern on Earth brought real knowledge of the human being into their circle through his intimate connection to spiritual speech. Hegel and Fichte could say:

> On Earth, we tried to fathom Earth's secrets, but there was no answer to the question before us in all that we gained from the deepest shafts of knowledge of Earth: What is the human being? In the whole cosmic context, what is the human being in reality? Come and explain to us what the human being is, what the human being brings us, and what the human being has already prepared for Heaven on Earth—a human being, a human star![95]

For souls who cross through the portal of death without having received thoughts about the Mystery of Golgotha while in the earthly body, the revealer was the human being who came up and whose soul was shone through fully by the light of what the new Christ revelation can be for the soul.[96]

That is the immense blessing: that Christian Morgenstern connected himself with the spirit of our movement and thus had the possibility of carrying it upward, so that those beings who had the desire to know such a thing could see Anthroposophy in the spiritual world.[97]

Rudolf Steiner did not go into further detail about the significance of Christian Morgenstern's spiritual life work for the spiritual world beyond this one. Nor did he give further details about the connection with the etheric Christ-being and his increasing visibility (and appearance) in the course of the twentieth century, which is stimulated and supported by the spiritual work of the Rosicrucians.[98] He presented only the direct effect on the dead of Morgenstern's consciousness, which had been illumined through Spiritual Science, and beyond that, the relevance of the "tableau" of cosmic imaginations he had created for the souls of the unborn who were prepared to incarnate or had begun to do so.

When Christian Morgenstern carried the Christ substance into the spiritual world with his pure being, he worked not only for his own spiritual progress, but also for that of all humanity. ("In this way…what such a soul has received serves not just his own soul, but is a possession that all humanity also has in common through Christ, who is present for all of humanity; it works, as well, on all of humanity."[99]) In this connection, Rudolf Steiner said about Christian Morgenstern and the unborn souls:

> Not only will our friend continue in his own life to carry on through perfected Anthroposophy for his own perfection, but by being received by the Christian world, it will also become an impulse from the spiritual world to those souls who will incarnate in the centuries to come; whatever is Christ-imbued will radiate into it.[100]

As he occasionally expressed, there is no doubt that the whole process Rudolf Steiner experienced and accompanied during the weeks and months after Christian Morgenstern crossed the threshold had great—the greatest—consequences for him. "*What I was allowed to experience in the spiritual worlds belongs to the deepest:* in this earthly incarnation, what I have striven to find in the spiritual worlds, had spread out over the realm of the higher world, like an artistic painting woven into Christian Morgenstern's spiritual garment."[101]

"Cosmic imaginations" in the spirit body of that friend were important for more than Rudolf Steiner's further spiritual work ("...[cosmic imaginations that] now radiate to the searching spiritual researcher and can explain much that he would otherwise not find as easily"[102]); more than this, Steiner placed great emphasis on the transformation process as such, pointing out that perception of the "soul tableau" in Christian Morgenstern's spirit body (that is, the metamorphosis of the earthly reception of anthroposophical teaching into a visible reality after death) "can instill trust for inner truth in a tremendous way and become the inner driving force of our movement."[103]

Christian Morgenstern wrote to Margareta from Budapest in early summer 1909 that he needed Rudolf Steiner as the "personally living guarantor, or assurance" for the "tremendous cosmic images" of Anthroposophy. Steiner was unaware of this formulation in his friend's letter, but five years later he said in Norrköping about the after-death development and appearance of Morgenstern:

> The cosmic tableau being developed for clairvoyant sight in the soul of the one who passed through the portal of death this spring—that Christ-imbued soul tableau is, for me, assurance that what may be spoken today from the spiritual worlds will, through Christ's love, shine down into souls that will come later. They will be set on fire and inspired by it.[104]

In a somewhat personal expression two months before Norrköping, in the Berlin Branch, which he had founded and developed himself, Rudolf Steiner indicated the actual importance of this experience for him during the difficult year of 1914, when, step-by-step, Central Europe was approaching the abyss of World War I and Anthroposophy, with its Dornach building, came under massive attack:

> People like this friend, whom you knew, become the best helpers to help Spiritual Science fulfill its task in the world. Since Spiritual Science is met in many quarters with misunderstanding, contempt, and hostility, we may feel that it will be truly difficult to make any progress toward achieving its real purpose. Nevertheless, the insights we have discussed today evoke the encouraging thought that those who have passed through the gate of death become true witnesses for the true nature and purpose of Spiritual Science. I would like this thought to speak to our hearts and souls.
>
> With this in mind, we cannot help believing that, even if it takes longer than our lifetime, Spiritual Science will become part of the spiritual progress of humanity. This thought can encourage us to face what confronts us in certain quarters; it can give us courage in our conviction that more and more people will come to see the need to develop new concepts, new ideas, sentiments, and attitudes, for a new understanding of the spiritual world.[105]

Thus, spiritual assistance was a reciprocal process between Christian Morgenstern and Rudolf Steiner, an "*unendingly intensified communion of beings*" or a "*conversation of the highest kind of mutual give-and-take*"—even though Morgenstern would have, from his great modesty, rejected this statement during his life. Many passages in Rudolf Steiner's lectures following Morgenstern's earthly death point out, with regard to this, that the spiritual friend and his assistance—despite the "deep unity" experienced even before the crossing of the threshold—became evermore essential for the progress of Anthroposophy and for the individual life of the one who had to represent it on Earth. They speak further to the fact that the mission of Christian Morgenstern's individuality could be recognized to its full extent, even for Rudolf Steiner, only after his friend had crossed the threshold. Steiner said, "We look up to him. We want to learn gradually—we want to recognize which important individuality was embodied in him.... After he has become ours—after we have recognized him—we will connect many things with this name."[106] Not only did he say this, but he also formulated a clearly personal expression on October 7, 1914, in the Dornach carpentry:

> It is one of the most shaking experiences one can have when one sees that he [Christian Morgenstern] lives his real, true being only now in the spiritual world. It is one of the most shattering experiences to see how this human being lived imprisoned by the most diverse impediments here in the physical world, and how this being—intuitively recognizable and able to be experienced by those who love this individual—can now freely unfold in the spiritual world. It is shocking that we cannot fully know such a being until we grasp his significance after death.[107]

Rudolf Steiner also stressed in a memorial talk for Christian Morgenstern (on September 20, 1914, the first anniversary of laying the Foundation Stone for the Dornach Johannes Building) that, for Christian Morgenstern, it appeared in such a living way before his soul; "how one can come to know human beings in an entirely different way than in physical life if one is in a position to behold them after they have left the physical plane."[108]

Margareta Morgenstern had written to the spiritual teacher from Moran in the very final period of the poet's life,

"Christian's thoughts are so much in Dornach."[109] According to Morgenstern's wish, a drawing of the main portal of the Johannes Building would be printed on the violet cover of *We Have Found a Path,* as if to say, "Whoever enters the feelings laid down in this book will find a way through the door by which one enters the Dornach Building."[110] Rudolf Steiner prepared the drawing according to Morgenstern's wish, but Reinhard Piper, Morgenstern's publisher, rejected such a cover design.

After his death, Christian Morgenstern remained connected with and accompanied the Dornach building further, as Rudolf Steiner stressed explicitly in his memorial address. This "accompaniment," without a doubt, referred not only to the Building but also to Rudolf Steiner and his path toward death in his studio on March 30, 1925. During the months following Christian Morgenstern's death, Rudolf Steiner spoke repeatedly about the support for the Mystery Dramas given by the individuality of Maria Strauch-Spettini, a teacher who had died at an early age and had been a friend of Marie Steiner-von Sivers.

> It was not as early as 1907, but from the time of our Mystery Dramas in Munich; from 1909 and then increasingly afterward, this soul was always present, guarding and clarifying what I could undertake for the Munich festival plays. Owing to its disposition in relation to beauty, what this soul was able to give to the artistic realization of our spiritual ideals worked down from the spiritual world, as though descending from the guardian angel of our Mystery Dramas, so that one felt within oneself the power to take the necessary initiative. Just as in the physical world our muscular energy supports us, so the spiritual force streaming down from the spiritual worlds flowed into

The Johannes Building (first Goethanum)
February 10, 1914

> one's own spiritual force. Thus the dead work and are present with us.[111]

How important the assistance of the individuality of Christian Morgenstern was for Rudolf Steiner' work from March 31, 1914 to March 30, 1925—and for the crowning of this work in the Christmas Conference—can be surmised only from the earthly perspective. Not the least, the culmination of Rudolf Steiner's mantric work took place completely during this time, including the ritual texts of the Movement for Religious Renewal, with which Margareta Morgenstern and Michael Bauer were deeply connected.

Rudolf Steiner had *We Have Found a Path,* Christian Morgenstern's volume of poetry, with him at the memorial address in the Dornach studio on September 20, 1914. In the copy intended for him, Margareta Morgenstern had placed, after the death of her husband and the book's publication, a small piece of paper on which were written six personal lines from Christian Morgenstern. In closing, Rudolf Steiner spoke of them.

> I do not want to recite the little poem that Margarita Morgenstern inserted into the copy of the poems intended for me. It was written by Christian Morgenstern in pencil in his beautiful handwritten strokes on May 13, 1912. However, without violating modesty, perhaps I may be permitted to share the last two lines of this unpublished poem in a particular connection—in connection with me. As stated, it is not from a lack of modesty that it is spoken, but because I want to speak about an esoteric fact—in connection with me, inasmuch as I have to represent this spiritual movement before Christian Morgenstern through my personality. In connection with that, the poem closes with the words:

> And inscribed into my fourfold form
> your cross as a silent support.
>
> *Und schrieb in mein Viergestalt*
> *ihr Kreuz wie einen stillen Halt.*
>
> Yes, my dear friends, it was one of the most beautiful and sublime, the most sublime task of our spiritual movement—to inscribe into this fourfold form the holy cross, the symbol of our movement, as a silent support. And now I must often find Christian Morgenstern by meditating. And these lines, along with those that precede them, always build, so to speak, what conveys the path to this soul. And, in many ways, this soul is to be found through meditation.[112]

At the beginning of May 1912 Christian Morgenstern wrote the following in pencil in the "Villa Silesia":

> Blessed I went into the world,
> cultivated my country by your hand.
>
> How often, since then, as comfort given,
> did this dear hand appear to me—
>
> and inscribe onto my fourfold form
> your Cross like a silent support.
>
> *Gesegnet ging ich in die Welt,*
> *mein Land von Deiner Hand bestellt.*
>
> *Wie oft seitdem, als Trostespfand,*
> *erschien mir diese liebe Hand—*
>
> *und schrieb in meine Viergestalt*
> *ihr Kreuz wie einen stillen Halt.*[113]

Rudolf Steiner, 1915

3

Easter 1915

Seven Poems by Christian Morgenstern

And just as Christ was the "Word," true Spiritual Science will work only through the Word, and must not work through anything else.[114]

On Palm Sunday 1915, just shy of one year after Christian Morgenstern's death, Rudolf Steiner held his last memorial address in the carpentry of the Johannes Building for the departed friend—an address with which Passiontide and the Easter Festival began amid World War I. In remembrance of that, Marie Steiner-von Sivers wrote, "Christian Morgenstern stands before Rudolf Steiner's soul as a human symbol of the deep Good Friday and Easter thought. He went through the festival of the Burial and the Resurrection together with a friend who stands, through death, so strongly with him in the true life."[115]

At the end of his address, Rudolf Steiner had seven poems by Christian Morgenstern recited (represented in this chapter). They are from the book *We Have Found a Path,* and contain a path to the Easter Mystery that should apparently accompany the members of the Anthroposophical Society during Passiontide. He ended his contemplations of Christian Morgenstern's significance in the spiritual world immediately before the recitation of verse:

> What he is and how he lives for the spirit land should stand here before the soul at the beginning of this week and should symbolize, in a festive way, the resurrection of life for us. May what our dear friend Christian Morgenstern is for the spirit land enter our hearts this week, so that our hearts may celebrate a festival of gratitude in mindfulness for the one who for years was in the midst of our spiritual-scientific stream for its fructification and enlivening, and of whom we may be certain that his entry to the spirit land—precisely through what he had developed in his soul in his final years—has become significant and deeply effective. I am interested only in the image that, for the spirit land and thus for us, is the image of the soul embodied in Christian Morgenstern. *May this image live in your hearts throughout the coming Easter week, and may what Christian Morgenstern embodied celebrate the resurrection in your hearts.* In grateful, holy reflection on Christian Morgenstern, especially during this week of his death, in this our Easter week, we want to develop the resurrection of our sensory impressions and feelings. May he himself speak to us in keeping with what he created here in earthly existence.[116]

Easter 1915

I thank you, mute stone,
and incline myself down to you;
I owe you my plant being.

I thank you, soil and plant,
and bend down to you;
you helped me to the animal.

I thank you, stone, herb, and animal,
and bow down to you;
You all helped all three of me to me.

We thank you, human child,
and reverently forsake ourselves before you;
because you are, we are.

Thanks flows from the one God—
and from all the diverse Divinity.
All being intertwined in gratitude.

Ich danke dir, du stummer Stein,
und neige mich zu dir hernieder:
Ich schulde dir mein Pflanzensein,

Ich danke euch, ihr Grund und Flor,
und bücke mich zu euch hernieder:
Ihr halft zum Tiere mir empor.

Ich danke euch, Stein, Kraut und Tier,
und beuge mich zu euch hernieder:
Ihr halft mir alle drei zu Mir.

Wir danken dir, du Menschenkind,
und lassen fromm uns vor dir nieder:
Weil dadurch, daß du bist, wir sind.

Es dankt aus aller Gottheit Ein—
und aller Gottheit Vielfalt wieder.
In Dank verschlingt sich alles Sein.[117]

The sheer want of a great good
is most certainly a high human striving.
Yet it does not achieve its full flowering,

until the grace of an awakened seer,
a soul emerged from night, has made conscious
the cosmos as a work of art created by spiritual beings.

Then, from an enormous survey of creation, there grows
from upward-directed vision of hidden sculpted spheres,
from inner participation in stages of the work—

sympathy and compassion for this world's destiny
nourishes more than the heart's dark urges;
the highest gods are called to work.

Das bloße Wollen einer großen Güte
ist ganz gewiß ein hohes Menschentrachten.
Doch es erhebt sich erst zur vollen Blüte,

wenn Gnaden eines seherisch Erwachten
den Kosmos nachtentleitetem Gemüte,
als Geisterkunstwerk zum Bewußtsein brachten.

Dann wächst aus Riesenschöpfungsüberblicken,
aus Aufschau zu verborgnen Bildnersphären,
aus Selbstmiteinbezug in deren Stufen—

ein Mitgefühl mit dieser Welt Geschicken,
das mehr als dunkle Herzenstriebe nähren,
das höchste Götter mit ans Werk berufen.[118]

I have seen the HUMAN in its deepest form;
I know the world, down to its deepest essence.
I know that Love, Love is its deepest meaning,
and that I am here to love, more and more.
I spread wide my arms as HE did,
and like HIM, I want to embrace the whole world.

Ich habe den MENSCHEN gesehn in seiner tiefsten Gestalt,
Ich kenne die Welt bis auf den Grundgehalt.
I weiß, daß Liebe, Liebe ihr tiefster Sinn,
und daß ich da, um immer mehr zu lieben, bin.
Ich breite die Arme aus , wie ER getan,
ich möchte die ganze Welt, wie ER, umfahn.[119]

Grasp what unveils itself to you!
Sense your way with prescience up to the Sun!
Sense the Creator's delight
that fills every being there!

Climb then these Spirits'
stages, up to the highest group!
And then finally see Him—
the Master of all these Spirits!

Then come down with him!
Among humans and demons
Come with him to live in the body
that a human being reverently gave for him.

Does a heart grasp the greatness of the sacrifice?
Can a spirit fully gauge this sacrifice?
How a God exchanges Heaven's radiance
for human need and nakedness!

Faß es, was sich dir enthüllt!
Ahne dich hinan zur Sonne!
Ahne, welche Schöpfer-Wonne
jedes Wesen dort erfüllt!

Klimm empor dann dieser Geister
Stufen bis zur höchsten Schar!
Und dann endlich nimm Ihn wahr:
Aller dieser Geister Meister!

Und dann komm mit Ihm herab!
Unter Menschen und Dämonen
Komm mit Ihm, den Leib bewohnen,
den ein Mensch Ihm fromm ergab.

Faßt ein Herz des Opfers Größe?
Mißt ein Geist dies Opfer ganz?
Wie ein Gott des Himmels Glanz
Tauscht um Menschennot und -blöße![120]

I am born from God like all that is;
I go into God with all that is mine to die;
I turn homeward, o God, to live as yours.

At first, I was given from your "I,"
then what was given had to be earned;
it had to be raised as you, breast to breast.

But right in the middle pride sought to corrupt it,
and it became you, and you were lost to pride...
until you powerfully called to me!

I was born to you a second time,
then I understood for the first time how to die;
then I felt for the first time what it was to live.

Ich bin aus Gott wie alles Sein geboren,
ich geh im Gott mit allem Mein zu sterben,
ich kehre heim, o Gott, als Dein zu leben.

Erst wurde ich aus Deinem Ich gegeben,
dann galt es dies Gegebene zu erwerben,
Dir als ein Du es Brust an Brust zu heben.

Da wollte Stolz es mittendrin verderben
und es ward Dir, und Du warst ihm verloren...
Biß daß Du übermächtig mich beschworen!

Da ward ich Dir zum andermal geboren:
denn ich verstand zum erstenmal zu sterben,
denn ich enpfand zum erstenmal zu leben.[121]

Now YOU live in it,
in this empty house,
from which the roaring world
has fled and gone.

What, then, is now still my significance—
Other than that, for a moment,
I am solely YOUR dwelling,
YOU, my foundation and my source!

Nun wohne DU darin,
in diesem leeren Hause,
aus dem der Welt Gebrause
herausfloh und dahin.

Was ist nun noch mein Sinn,—
Als daß auf eine Pause
ich einzig DEINE Klause,
mein Grund und Urspung bin![122]

I raise my heart to you
as a true Grail chalice
that lost all its blood in thirst
after your pure Supper,
    O CHRIST!

O fill it anew right to the brim
with your blood's rosy blaze,
so that I carry IT from now on
through earthly nights and days,
    YOU are!

Ich hebe Dir mein Herz empor
als rechte Gralesschale,
das all sein Blut im Durst verlor
nach Deinem reinen Mahle,
    O CHRIST!

O füll es neu bis an den Rand
mit Deines Blutes Rosenbrand,
daß: DEN fortan ich trage
durch Erdennächt' und -tage,
    DU bist![123]

"The Slavic Human" by Rudolf Steiner; pastel study for painting the small cupola of the Johannes Building, Dornach 1914

Epilogue

"Of all the languages, I actually understood only—Russian..."

Christian Morgenstern and the Spiritual Russia

Michael Bauer, who was Christian Morgenstern's great friend and an anthroposophical companion in his final year of life, was loved by the Russian anthroposophists around the Johannes Building and was considered to be part of their circle. Andrei Bely described Bauer as the "natural patron" of the Russians in Dornach/Arlesheim, where Michael Bauer stayed for a little less than three years, from the beginning of January 1915, in the company of Margareta Morgenstern. In Arlesheim, he lived in the same house as Trifon Georgiewitsch Trapeznikov and was part of the anthroposophical community around Rudolf Steiner in the carpentry of the building during the Eastertide of 1915.

> Master Eckhart of our century—
> I remember how you from Arlesheim to Dornach
> passed by us in a time of consternation.
> You came, bowing in blossoms and thorns.
>
> (Andrei Bely).[124]

It was not Andrei Bely but indeed Michael Chekhov who would be (along with Margareta Morgenstern) with Michael Bauer as he died fourteen years later on June 18, 1929, when he received yet a final blessing from him: "Courage, Mischa, courage—we are in battle! With Christ you will find courage."[125] A while before that, at Chekhov's request, Michael Bauer had written an extensive letter about Russia's future (the end of the letter no longer exists):

> You ask about Russia's destiny. I think Dr. Steiner did not say anything specific about the near future, but only about the more distant future. You know that. There is a report from him that the occultists in the West (the political–imperialistic brotherhoods) saw that they could no longer cope with the social impulses in European humanity. They decided to create an area for experimentation where the social impulses (that are, from their point of view, only utopias) should develop fully and lead to absurdity. For them, this field for experimentation is Russia. The great social impulses that live in modern humanity (especially in the proletariat and in Russia naturally) were blocked by Marxism and were distorted by it. Basically, they are the most spiritual soul forces, but are prevented materialistically. And one allows these distorted social impulses to live fully in the East, to show how absurd all socialism is!
>
> With that, one wants to generate antipathy against all social movements and ideals. This experiment will continue as long as those Western brotherhoods consider it to be necessary. Freely, it is already beginning to become more than they can handle, because through it the Asian people are becoming restless. However, the actual blame for all of this disaster lies in the West. (Someone should once put together everything that Rudolf Steiner said about Russia.) I want to mention yet another point of view.

(It is nowhere to be found with Dr. Steiner; it comes to light from spiritual scientific contemplation.")

You know that there is an etheric geography and that, accordingly, in every area of the Earth there are different etheric effects that then work back on the people and culture at any given time. In Russia the pure Light Ether works particularly strongly; it does not work directly, however, but in its reflection from the Earth. In this way the Russian person takes it in. The Russian takes in the heavenly in the mirror of the Earth—the light aspect indirectly from the ground. This is why the Russian person loves the Earth so deeply, loves it as something that rays out the heavenly. The Earth does not make a person materialistic, nor does the heavenly make one despise the Earth. That is the uniquely favorable aspect of the Russian soul disposition. (It is something else that certain streams have *made* of the Russian today. On the one side is the Eastern mystical impulse that has worked through centuries and wants to make the Russian an ascetic; on the other side is the Western intellectualism that wants the Russian to deny the heavens: the luciferic and ahrimanic temptations. Because the luciferic worked so strongly through the centuries, now the Russian is attacked so strongly.)

Now at this time, however, something special comes in addition. With the Resurrection of Christ in the etheric realm something like an immense agitation begins, yes, a revolution in the whole etheric realm of the Earth: "And the sea and the waves will roar" (Luke 21:25). An immense brewing or building-up process is occurring in all the elemental spheres. Through this, however, countless droves of elemental spirits become awake and begin to stir. The elemental spirits yearn for the new light that flows through the whole surroundings of the Earth from the Christ resurrecting in the etheric realm. One must imagine how they begin to glisten and shine in this wonderful aura of light rays that builds around the Earth from now on. Through the particular kind of etheric effects in the Russian region of the Earth—of which we spoke before—this shining and developing of the elemental kingdoms already now begins to a quite special degree in the European East. Yes, it has already begun; it is only that people do not yet notice it. Human beings will always become aware of the shining forth of the spiritual much later than the demons. (These also recognized Christ in the flesh earlier! [Mark 1:24]).

Ahrimanic beings (demons) always have an extreme greed for the golden, shining astral light wherever it becomes visible. They become absolutely wild about possessing this light treasure. (Consider the Rheingold that Alberich steals and seizes for himself.) Now I want and dare to express something I cannot prove intellectually. Ahrimanic beings of Earth saw the particular area of Earth where especially the shining of elemental kingdoms has already begun and where the new Christ light has spread out over the whole sphere like the red sky before sunrise. They saw this shining treasure, this aura of light rays, and therefore gathered together over Russia. They pounced on this shining etheric sphere and ate, as it were, the glowing elemental beings. They devour the golden light hoard. However, there is one thing that demons do not know. They do not know the deeper effect of this astral–etheric light. It has the power to dissolve and disperse *from within* everything that is dark and condensed. Thus working from within, the devoured light dissolves the condensed, compressed bodies of the demons' phantoms.

One can imagine this as a chemical-spiritual process, thus paralyzing or laming the demonic powers. With this, however, the devoured astral light (working further in a hidden way) purifies the Earth's atmosphere. This is a powerful effect of Christ in the etheric realm, as I see it. Now we are already in the midst of this process. The pressing together of the demons over the severely tested

Russia, as well as their destructive work there, receive thus a completely new aspect that is naturally understandable only to esotericists. Once one understands this, one also knows that the paralyzing, demon-dissolving power of Christ is also already effective, and that it shines through and dissolves those shadow powers in the etheric realm. This is a powerful event that has now begun to take place. Thus one can get an idea from a completely different side of the deeper occurrences in everything that, considered from the earthly side, looks so dark and hopeless: Russia's destiny.

Dear Mr. Chekhov, I write here to you several indications of something that I have never expressed before. It is understood that these last ones are not from Dr. Steiner. However, I believe it is nevertheless something that, based on Spiritual Science, I may express as true. For now, just take it as a picture, and you will be able to feel your way into it and sense whether it is true or not. You can imagine that this must all be a significant experience for the folk spirit of Russia, the archangel, for the archangel sees this, too, and goes through it himself. However, what happens because of this? He enters very rapid development. It is a kind of initiation that he goes through there. He matures rapidly and imbues himself with Christ and pushes the demonic itself from himself. Freely, an ahrimanic counter-spirit forms first of all through this—a dark double of the folk spirit, for it is not only human beings that have doubles. This ahrimanic counter-spirit wants to make human beings with no "I." He wants to form them into mere masses (Bolshevism).

Thus, one can imagine that, from now on, always to a special degree—more intensively than with other peoples—this archangel will have a double, an ahrimanic distorted picture, beside him. Through this, however, he also comes to know this being—a bearer of the strongest antichrist impulse—even better. He must continue to live with

> it and wrestle with it until he gradually conquers it after a long time. (In the cupola of the old Goetheanum the Russian human being was depicted as a double figure. From now on, this is also true for the archangel.) The Russian archangel will, in that he must now experience this destiny in advance, so that in a...[the text ends here][126]

≈

Michael Bauer accompanied and helped many Russian friends among the anthroposophists in inner and outer crises. Among them was the painter Margarita Woloschin, who experienced his spiritual help during her life-threatening illness with typhoid fever in 1919/20 in postrevolutionary devastated Russia. "One time as I thought about Michael Bauer, his being was so quickly present that I feared that he could have died in the meantime and that I was meeting his soul. At the same time, Michael Bauer—as he told me later—beheld me lying in torn sheets and thought that I must be severely ill."[127] Like Rudolf Steiner, Michael Bauer supported in Germany—in spite of his severe tuberculosis that kept him from working further on the Executive Council of the Anthroposophical Society—not only the teachers' collegium in the Stuttgart School and the young priest group of The Christian Community in a spiritual and social way ("Rudolf Steiner himself referred us to him, and him to us" [Rittelmeyer][128]), but, beyond this, many people both living and dead. Alexander Strakosch described Michael Bauer's task as, "to establish the connection between the realm of the dead and that of the living."[129] Bauer himself wrote in an essay:

> True Christianity strives for the penetration of earthly life with heavenly being—that transformation of the

> Earth as is stated in the petitions of the *Our Father.* To the degree that Christianity attains form, equally it will change the fundamental mood of human earthly life in relation to the life of the dead. We will feel ourselves as cosmic spirit beings in the mortal body and sense existence. In our doing, something of the creative heavenly world's joy of becoming will be present. Then, however, the Christian soul that is incarnated and the Christian souls that have crossed through the portal of death will know themselves to be ever closer to each other and will work together ever more consciously. Among the tasks of our self-education will then be, of course, that we learn how we truly remain loyal to our dead and how we prepare our consciousness in that respect so that it is no longer unreceptive to their loyalty.[130]

Like Rudolf Steiner, Michael Bauer remained inseparably connected with Christian Morgenstern after March 31, 1914. He made impressive statements repeatedly about this living connection.[131] Although his own inner sight was directed mainly toward the further activity of Morgenstern's individuality in the spiritual world, Bauer and Margareta Morgenstern took care of ordering and penetrating Christian Morgenstern's estate. He worked for many years, with the last of his strength, on writing his biography, mostly during his fever-free hours at night. "Oh, if only I had finished the biography so that I might be allowed to cast off this worn-out body!"[132] Along with Rudolf Steiner, Michael Bauer knew the significance of writing a biography for the success of taking up a relationship with the great individualities of the spiritual world. He wanted to work in this sense for the future with his description of Christian Morgenstern's life. When Bauer died, his book was not yet completed. Four years after his death, it would be published with

Morgenstern's publisher Reinhard Piper in Munich after Margareta Morgenstern and Rudolf Meyer completed it.

In his extensive study of the biography of his friend, Michael Bauer portrayed an accurate picture of Morgenstern's soul-spiritual and literary development. He was thus able to, among other things, describe that "breakthrough through the Johannine," which Christian Morgenstern experienced at the sanitarium in Birkenwerder, Germany during the winter of 1905/06, in his thirty-fifth year of life—*"since I found me in myself."*[133] Michael Bauer illumined and made comprehensible Morgenstern's spiritual experiences at this turning point in his biography. With this, he showed the extent to which Morgenstern's draft of his novel *Tagebuch eines Mystiker* [diary of a mystic], as well as his series of poems *"Der Christus"* [the Christ], were related to the Birkenwerder experiences of Johannine Christianity and the higher "I." He also described Morgenstern's deep encounter with the spiritual Russia at that time.

Christian Morgenstern withdrew from all the other guests at the Sanitarium of Birkenwerder and talked a lot with three Jewish women—a mother and her two daughters, who were also there. According to Bauer, he read with them—with the greatest interest—from Dostoyevsky's final work, *The Brothers Karamazov* (as well as from the memoirs of Peter Kropotkin). He noted that, from Dostoyevsky's books, one has a hard time finding a way back to Western Europe.[134] According to Bauer, Morgenstern expected the "new Word" of the future to come from the spirituality of Russia. In the spiritual deepening and turning of the Johannine-imbued winter months in Birkenwerder, Russians seemed to him to be, by far, the most Christian people on Earth.[135]

Although Christian Morgenstern reluctantly left the retreat space of the sanitarium and its rural environs in the winter and largely avoided Berlin, in February and March 1906 he nevertheless attended guest performances of the Moscow Art Theater in Berlin. He saw and was deeply impressed by, among others, pieces by Aleksey Tolstoy, Anton Chekhov, and Maxim Gorky. He said:

> One felt that something was there that one did not have oneself. Experts attributed it to the great number of Stanislavski rehearsals. Yet, can one, through however many rehearsals, actually convey something of the mood that came from individual scenes involving "Uncle Vanya" or the "Three Sisters?"... What was it, however, that one does not have oneself and that streamed out so strongly, precisely from the Chekhov scenes? A breath of the Slavic soul, the Slavic spirit, and at that, a soul and spirit that stands closer to the future than we do... not America, but Russia is the land of unlimited opportunity.[136]

Two years later, Morgenstern nevertheless investigated the enchantment that arose from the Berlin performances of the Moscow theater troupe around Konstantin Sergeievich Stanislavski. Even the Berlin critics and reviewers Siegfried Jacobsohn and Alfred Kerr could not evade that enchantment, describing their final reason as being the "love" they felt there. "Love, love to one another, to us, to their poets—wordless, unexpressed, unacknowledged, yet self-evident love. There is no other word for it—at the most, one could say 'inner religiosity.' The final beauty of this artist poured forth from this."[137] Morgenstern spoke of a "more profound seriousness" and of a more mature humanity that characterized the Russian artists.[138] Even before his encounter with Anthroposophy, he looked expectantly toward Eastern

Europe, especially Russia, without giving in to political illusions. Nevertheless, he looked for the future of culture, consciousness, and human soul forces on the way to the spirit. At the end of May 1909, he wrote a remarkable statement to Margareta from Budapest about the opening of the Congress of the Federation of the European Sections of the Theosophical Society. The sentence read, "*How nice it would have been for you. Of all the languages there, I actually understood only Russian. I felt that this would someday be my future native tongue.*"[139]

In Anthroposophy, or in Rudolf Steiner's spiritual-scientific lectures and writings, Christian Morgenstern found, in the final years of his life, statements about this "future mother tongue" and the home sphere that confirmed his expectations and more. Rudolf Steiner described the future task of Russia as the cultural development of humanity and characterized the special foundations and capabilities of the Russian folk soul and the Russian folk spirit for this leading role.[140] However, Morgenstern most likely had no opportunity to read the notes or written copies of Rudolf Steiner's addresses directly to the Russian anthroposophists in April 1912 and June 1913 in Helsinki.[141] There Steiner presented in outline not only a succinct condensation of the spiritual history of the Theosophical/Anthroposophical Society and movement, which was contentious from the beginning, but also spoke of the special tasks of the Russian folk soul for the future of modern Spiritual Science and the evolution of civilization. Among other things, he said at the time:

> The spiritual that is in this Theosophy [or Anthroposophy] can…be found by souls that thirst and long for it. And

here I must say, my dear theosophical friends, that I myself have become acquainted, from the spiritual world, with a soul that has a great longing for the spirit that comes to expression through Theosophy. I came to know this soul in the true spiritual world. When we ascend in the sequence of the hierarchies to the individual folk spirits and speak among the various folk spirits about the folk souls, we come, among the folk souls that are, so to speak, still young and must evolve further—as every folk soul must—to the Russian folk soul. I know that this Russian folk soul longs for the spirit expressed in Theosophy. It longs for it with all the forces that it can develop.

I am speaking about a sense of responsibility, because you, my dear theosophical friends, are children of this Russian folk soul. It exerts its power and influence within you, and you have a responsibility toward it. Learn this responsibility! Do not take this the wrong way, but this Russian folk soul could often tell me many, many things, the most tragic of which is what the Russian folk soul was able to tell me sometime around the year 1900. It appeared in a particularly tragic light at that time, because what was noticeable then was something I could not interpret correctly until long afterward—that this Russian folk soul is still understood to only a very limited degree today.

In Western Europe we have learned a great deal from Russia, and there is much that has made an enormous impression upon us. We have become familiar with the great impulses of Tolstoy, the deep psychological insights of Dostoyevsky, and finally the spirit of Solovyov, a spirit who—when we let him work on us—always gives the impression everywhere that what he writes is who he is. Moreover, we do not see his writings in their true light unless we sense the Russian folk soul standing behind him. This Russian folk soul has far more to say than Solovyov himself knows to say, as far too much from Western Europe comes to meet us in what he says.

Think, my dear friends, of this "sense of responsibility" and call to mind that you have the task of making yourselves worthy of the Russian folk soul and that you need to recognize its longing for...Theosophy. When you come to know what theosophy wants in its innermost impulse, you will have all kinds of questions that can come only from a Russian soul—questions that address the spiritual questions of Theosophy. I have experienced so many noble, lofty and beautiful feelings that have come toward me from Eastern Europe; so much true human love and goodness, compassion and overflowing feelings that can be ascribed only to a fine, intimate observation of what lives in the world, an intensely personal relationship with the ruling powers of existence. And from such loving and beautiful and noble feelings, many questions have been asked of me by those belonging to the Russian people—questions that must be asked, because they are questions that, unless they are answered, humanity will not be able to live in the future. Questions that can come only from Eastern Europe have until now been posed to me only by the Russian folk soul on higher planes.

Often I had to think that the children of this folk soul still have a long way to go before they understand their folk soul, before they understand what this folk soul really longs for and how much still separates them from it. Do not, therefore, hold back from seeking the path to your folk soul, for you will find it, if you want it. It is from your folk soul that you will discover those questions that must be answered if humanity is to exist in the future. Do not be afraid of reaching beyond personal interests, for you need to be mindful of the great responsibility that you have toward the Russian folk soul.

In the future, the folk souls will need their children, the human beings, to attain their objectives. And do not forget one thing. That power which can support a person at the highest level and can lead him or her to the

> most beautiful and most radiant heights of the world is most exposed to the danger of succumbing to errors. You should, my dear theosophical friends, imbue the spiritual with soul. You should find the way of the soul to the spirit. You can do this because the Russian folk soul has infinite depths and possibilities for the future. However, it is necessary that you are aware that the soul element—which can lift itself to the spirit and thus to pervade it—exposes you to the great danger of losing yourself in the purely personal element and of being stuck in it. Then the personal becomes strong.[142]

Rudolf Steiner told the Russian anthroposophists that the Russian folk soul could absorb modern Spiritual Science "as no other people could... like something you might care for and nurture as your own."[143] Russia, or the Russian souls, would have the possibility to imbue the spiritual world with soul, to fill the spirit with soul; that means not only to take in Anthroposophy intellectually, but to unite it with the soul and heart and thereby, at the same time, to build an intensive spiritual community through the joining together of hearts. In the West, acceptance of Anthroposophy was always confronted by the forces of skepticism and cynicism, of doubt and mockery, as Rudolf Steiner would later say in his Esoteric Lessons in Dornach. This danger does not exist in this way in Russia. There, however, exists the very real possibility, according to Rudolf Steiner, that "powerful emotional" aspects of the personality could distort "objective spirituality," rendering it alienating.

Rudolf Steiner spoke to the predominantly young Russian anthroposophists in Helsinki as teacher, helper, and friend. He told them that, especially in Russia, it is important to develop "energy and endurance," to transform suffering into strength and to aim for a strong "inner composure." It is much easier for the Russian soul than for the Western human being to enliven the "Christ impulse" in the heart—a process upon which Anthroposophy depends in the Michaelic Age. There exists also, however, the danger of a soul—centered on and characterized by emotion—to stray from this path in the direction of chaos and error. The Russian folk soul, however, has taken on a duty in relation to humanity and looks expectantly to its bearer. "I am speaking of your folk soul that is truly present in the spiritual world, awaiting its future task full of expectation, hope, and confidence."[144] Working intensively with Anthroposophy and internalizing it is not alone a question of personal joy and of a "personal longing"; in Russia it is much more a matter of understanding that the modern Spiritual Science is something "that present day humanity needs, if the evolution process of humanity is to proceed further at all."[145] If this reception of Anthroposophy were not to succeed, then the future of the Earth and humanity would clearly be hopeless.

> I say this for the simple reason that all the spiritual impulses of the past that have been given to humanity are exhausted. They have gradually fulfilled their tasks and are unable to bring new seeds for human evolution. If only the old impulses were to continue to have an influence, the future would inevitably be one in which technology of a purely external kind would not only overpower and outwardly overwhelm human beings to an unprecedented degree, but would paralyze them and take them over, even to the point of utter destruction, because it would draw from the human soul everything of a religious, scientific, philosophical and artistic nature, and also ethical interest in the higher sense. The human being would become a kind of living automaton if new spiritual impulses were not to come.[146]

Rudolf Steiner asked the Russian anthroposophists to feel "responsible" in this sense for Anthroposophy and to develop a sufficient consciousness of the significance of its impulse. Through Anthroposophy, "something completely new" must "flow into human evolution."[147] It is an essential task of Russia in the future to collaborate in this process and thereby to prepare responsibly the next cultural epoch of "spirit self." "*Then the time will come when Europe begins—and when you fulfill your duties in relation to your folk soul—to understand a little of what the Christ impulse actually is in the spiritual development of humanity.*"[148]

Looking back at Christian Morgenstern's life and work, his whole appearance and his way of working with Anthroposophy, it is clear that he bore within himself in his incarnation at the end of the nineteenth and beginning of the twentieth century, the real, concrete hope that Rudolf Steiner connected with the future Slavic-determined cultural epoch of "spirit self." As Rudolf Steiner emphasized again and again after Morgenstern's death, Christian Morgenstern was able to "imbue the spiritual intensively with soul" and really to unite Anthroposophy with his heart. He succeeded in transforming anthroposophic ideas "into personal feelings," but then carried everything personal up into the "supra-personal sphere" without losing his soul. It was important to him from the beginning that the Christ impulse should connect with modern Spiritual Science. Moreover, his entire devotion and commitment to Anthroposophy arose from a deep "feeling of responsibility"—an effective, long-lasting impulse of conscience in relation to the future of humanity and creation, which Rudolf Steiner mentioned briefly when he spoke in Finland. In his path of development, Morgenstern had for a long time already gone beyond the soul dangers just described, or they never confronted him. Despite all the capability for spiritual enthusiasm, he manifested a deeply impressive order, trained discipline, and unusually developed powers of will that—in spite of countless hindrances of the time and his own body—allowed him to move forward in a purposeful, goal-oriented way. In addition to the fire of his love of the spirit, he also bore within himself highly developed formative forces. The Grail mood that Rudolf Steiner ascribed to the spiritual Russia lived in him in an impressive way, however. It was connected with a clear intellect trained by philosophy, and with moral purity and impressive social skills that bore the "good spirit of brotherhood" and worked directly as community-building (his "love-awakening community soul"[149]). The spiritual community of a coming cultural epoch of the "spirit self" founded in the substance of love—as an Age of Morality and Love (R. Steiner)—had in him a herald and first representative.

Just a few months before his death, Christian Morgenstern met the Russian poet Andrei Bely, who followed, like no other anthroposophist, Rudolf Steiner's Christology lectures on the Fifth Gospel with intensity, spiritual wakefulness, and yes, passion. No doubt Bely had the soul potential that Rudolf Steiner described in Helsinki, but he was also fully bound up in its dangers. He recognized in Christian Morgenstern a highly developed brother. With all their differences, he—who was gifted with a marked sensibility—experienced a deep common bond of the heart with Christian Morgenstern:

> His smile radiated to me, and he pointed to his throat at the same time, indicating that he could no longer speak. He could say only hoarsely, "It pleases me.... It pleases me, but I cannot speak." We stood facing each other, smiled and squeezed each other's hands. One could think that this is not much, but we (he and I) both stood in those days precisely "on the mountaintop," both of us borne aloft in the same way by the lecture cycle *Christ and the Spiritual World*. I felt that there was no curtain [between us]; two inner worlds touched each other, almost unveiled. I am convinced of this even today. I do not know what Morgenstern saw in me, but what flowed from him to me can be compared to a hot stream of light that covered me like a cloak and led the soul, for a moment, into the *Hut*. (I would most like to have called out, "Let's build a Hut!"). He radiated power before which the power of a usual esotericist is a nothing. The power of the Christ impulse went through me as a gust of wind; it drove right through me. As the Doctor spoke later about the power in Morgenstern that made him an "invisible helper" after his death, I was not surprised thinking about that moment when I stood before him with his hand in mine and I looked, not into a pair of eyes, but into the depths of heaven.[150]

Michael Bauer was present at this meeting and wrote about it later: "They held out their hands to each other, looked warmly at each other, but spoke no words. One lacks the strength to bring sound through his voice, and the other younger one, due to being inwardly moved, lacks the German words. Yet this was most expressive and the richest meeting between two human beings."[151] It was no longer possible for Christian Morgenstern (in contrast to Michael Bauer) to accompany on Earth such a highly gifted, though endangered, human being and Russian student of Rudolf Steiner such as Andrei Bely. He had to leave his earthly body as the work on the Dornach Johannes Building actually began, and as many young Russians arrived there. Yet the brief earthly meeting was essential as a prerequisite for what would come later, and Andrei Bely was still overjoyed at having met Christian Morgenstern. He looked into Morgenstern's eyes—"into the depths of heaven"—and grasped that he had met not only a special human being and poet, but also a herald of the future. In him he recognized a person who felt the joy and the pain of the other as his own. This means he was imbued with the spirit of brotherhood—was a Johannine Christian for whom the true meeting was a religious deed, or "sacrament," and who had a unique connection to the modern Spiritual Science of Anthroposophy.[152] Christian Morgenstern was not a Russian soul, but had a great love and a real understanding for it and its future task. Because of this, meeting with him was already health-giving and progressive.

The last "Hut" that Christian Morgenstern found on Earth in which to die in peace—after all the sanatoria that had refused to accept him—was in Merano, Maia Bassa. The owner, Frau von Ludwigowska, who came from Poland, allowed Margareta Morgenstern to rent a room after she, too, had looked into the eyes of the deathly ill poet. Margareta Morgenstern reported to Michael Bauer that she had said, "Only two times in my life have I seen such a look, such an expression in the eyes—with Christian Morgenstern and Johannes von Kronstadt."[153] Morgenstern felt in no way connected with the Russian Orthodox Church, but he lived toward a coming, Slavic-characterized cultural epoch of the "spirit self" and a Johannine Christianity. And he knew much about the "future Mysteries of the Holy Grail," for which he worked and prepared himself further.

On November 9, 1914, in Dornach—three months after the beginning of World War I and a little more than seven months after Christian Morgenstern's death—Rudolf Steiner described how, in the spiritual world, Michael fought for the approaching etheric Christ. He fought for the "purity of the spiritual horizon," against all deceptions and subjective imaginations of humanity and, according to Rudolf Steiner, is supported in this by human souls who are in the after-death world and are especially close to their own angels (or bear angel-consciousness within themselves), because they last went through a Russian incarnation.[154]

There is much to suggest that Christian Morgenstern—who felt himself "electively related" to spiritual Russia and its future task—was and remains of special, even outstanding, importance in Michael's centuries-long commitment to the approach of the etheric Christ. He carried Christianized Anthroposophy into the spiritual world. According to Rudolf Steiner, it could "become an impulse for the souls that will come alive in the coming centuries"; "they will be fired up inwardly; they will be inspired by it."

≈

During the same year (1914) in which the collaboration between Central and Eastern Europe experienced a disastrous and consequential break, Rudolf Steiner painted the pastel drawing "The Slavic Human" as a study for the later painting of the small cupola of the Johannes Building (see page 72). In 1989 (seventy years after the death of Michael Bauer and eighty-five years after Christian Morgenstern's departure from Earth), Sergei O. Prokofieff[155] wrote:

"The Slavic Human with Double, Angel, and Centaur," created by Rudolf Steiner in 1914 in pastel, is one of the most fully developed and artistically finished studies in preparation for the painting of the small cupola of the first Goetheanum. In his lecture of January 25, 1920, Rudolf Steiner said in connection with this motif: "One could only illustrate what was intended here by giving form and color to an initiate—that means to such a human being into whom the spiritual revelations of the future sixth post-Atlantean cultural period enter in, and to whom it already now comes as a prelude."[156] In other words, it is a matter here of a presentation not so much of today, but rather of the future representative of the sixth cultural epoch. One could also say that this study presents, in a certain way, the youth (prince) whose initiation J. W. von Goethe relates in his fairytale, "The Green Snake and the Beautiful Lily."

In this sketch, the Slavic human is at the bottom, at the base of the vertical symmetry axis of the composition. The Slavic human is painted completely in the color of a peach blossom, the color that, in the physical world, comes the closest to the suprasensory "color" of the human etheric body.[157] Indicated with this is the future clairvoyant character of the sixth cultural epoch.[158] For the natural, etheric clairvoyance that will then exist in all of humanity, the entire world will appear as a universal whole that encompasses the material world, as well as the spiritual world in a single higher synthesis and a harmonic balance at the same time. This synthesis is depicted in the sketch by the large, egg-shaped, or heart-shaped, form that encompasses the whole composition and gives it a character of being self-contained and resting in itself. It is also an indication of the "self-contained soul" that was already spoken of as a characteristic of all Slavic people.[159] At the same time, this powerful auric form is an imagination of the purified and transformed soul (astral body) of future Slavic human beings[160] who are prepared to take into themselves the substance of spirit self.

In the threefold being of the human, the soul lives and works between the principle of the spirit and the principle of the body. For this reason the auric form on the one side is restricted by the world of matter (the dark field on the right), and on the other side it opens itself to the left (as seen from the observer) and upward to the higher world of the divine spiritual hierarchies. These are represented by the angel figure on the left side. Its blue color points to the perfected will, devoted to the divine world—the will that Slavic human beings shall someday develop from their soul depths as striving toward a concrete formation of the future of the Earth, for the transformation of all material, and to its penetration with the spiritual.[161] The figure of the angel itself gives witness to the special relationship that the Eastern Slavic person has especially to this spiritual hierarchy closest to the human world. Rudolf Steiner said, "For members of the Russian folk it is natural always to be together with their angel."[162] However, whereas this relationship in today's fifth epoch develops mainly beyond the threshold of consciousness of the Eastern European and comes to full consciousness only after death, during the sixth epoch, with its new clairvoyance, this connection with the angel will already be experienced directly on the Earth itself, and with full consciousness. The whole egg-shaped auric form is filled with a golden sheen, similar to the golden background that one finds in most Byzantine and Russian icons. In them the gold is the symbol for the divine spiritual world from which the physical-earthly world proceeds. In contrast, in Rudolf Steiner's sketch it is an imaginative picture for the spiritual substance radiating from the higher worlds and gradually filling the whole soul space (astral body).

With his fairytale and description of the initiation of the youth in the Temple of Higher Knowledge, Goethe already pointed to the central role of the Golden King, who placed the oaken crown on the head of the youth with a gesture of fatherly blessing, saying, "Know the highest!" Goethe continues, "But as the oaken crown adorned his hair, his countenance was enlivened; his eyes shone with inexpressible spirit, and the first word from his mouth was "Lily." This "inexpressible *spirit*" that shone from his eyes is the "'I'-building and 'I'-living spirit" we can call "spirit self," because it appears as the human "I," or Self.[163] Because he was gifted with this, the youth was able to reach the Lily—the representative of the new "clairvoyant consciousness."[164]

This is also the reason Rudolf Steiner characterized in many lectures the Golden King as a bearer of the forces of the world wisdom, *manas,* or spirit self. "The Golden King is *manas*, the wisdom itself, which until now could develop further only in the Mystery Temple."[165] And in another place he said, "Through the Golden King the youth receives the knowledge in its most perfect form, *manas.* Now the marriage with the beautiful Lily may take place."[166] In a later lecture on December 8, 1918, he characterized the three kings of the fairytale as the representatives of Western, Central, and Eastern Europe. Rudolf Steiner was pointing to the connection between the Golden King and the last one: "The Russian is connected with what is signified as the third power, according to Goethe's fairytale, with the knowledge, or wisdom, that should arise in the sixth post-Atlantean age of humanity."[167] That is the higher wisdom that reveals itself in the suprasensory worlds as Light. Rudolf Steiner said, "Wisdom is spiritual Light."[168]

The radiant golden spiritual substance that fills the whole soul space of the future Eastern Slavic human has a source clearly expressed in the sketch. These are the head, the raised left hand, and the upper ends of the angel's wings that emanate a golden glow that is brighter and more intense than the general golden ground of the auric egg. It can also be said that this forms, as it were, a continuation of the figure and gestures of the angel. Like a powerful stream, this brighter, more intense golden glow pours from above to below along the right boundary (from the observer) of the egg-shaped form, whereby it becomes steadily weaker toward the bottom. Yet it protects the soul life of the Slavic human being from the penetrating of the forces of the outer darkness, the matter and the death (the dark field underneath and to the right of the boundary of the auric form that increasingly passes over further in the painting of the cupola into the dark profile of Ahriman). This stream fades somewhat at the level of the Slavic human being's hands holding the cross with the roses, connecting him directly with the sphere of the angel. The appearance of the spirit-self substance of a being that belongs to the hierarchy of the angels corresponds exactly with Rudolf Steiner's words: "Our 'I' must meet that higher, spirit self, which we will first develop [in the sixth cultural epoch] and has, in a certain sense, the same nature as those beings of the hierarchy of the angels."[169]

To achieve such a fully conscious meeting with the spirit self in the sixth epoch, every Slavic person must overcome two opposing forces that threaten the proper development of his or her soul. That is, on the one side, the ahrimanic double that has arisen through the penetrating of the forces of darkness, matter, and death into the soul from outside. In the sketch, the double is depicted as a direct continuation of the outer darkness, as a result of its flowing in or seeping into the inner essence of the auric egg. And on the other side, there is the danger of the darkening of the soul horizon through an unclear luciferic astrality that hinders the connection with the objective spirit. It is depicted in the sketch in the figure of the winged, fire-red centaur. Rudolf Steiner repeatedly calls this, in his lectures about the painting of the small cupola, "a kind of air centaur."[170] This is a reference to its astral nature, because air is an expression in the sense world of the astral element.[171] In his first lecture for the Russians[172] Rudolf Steiner characterized the principal soul danger that awaits the Russian on his or her path to the spirit, and on the historical plane on the path to the sixth cultural epoch in the following way: "Your danger will be that the mighty soul essence of your personalities can spread astral clouds around you that prevent you from reaching through to the objective spiritual realm. Your fire, your warmth, can gather around you like a cloudy aura and not let the spiritual come through. You think you are really enthusiastic for the spirit, but this very enthusiasm prevents the spirit from finding its way to you."[173] In an imaginative form, the figure of the centaur in the sketch represents the danger that exists between the Russian people and the golden spirit substance that flows gradually from above as a "objective spiritual" element into their astral aura. Moreover, the form of the centaur characterizes the duality of human nature in the fifth cultural epoch; it "contains the human being, on the one side, but, on the other, also contains the lower animal nature within the human being." Therefore, it can actually be said, "To a certain extent, the human being is really a centaur." Rudolf Steiner speaks about this in his lecture of November 25, 1917,[174] and points out that certain esoteric circles or "brotherhoods" of Indo–Tibetan occultists will attempt to use this duality in order to lead especially Eastern Europe astray spiritually. "That is that dualism of forces that will be used more by certain egotistical brotherhoods of the Eastern Indian stream in order to tempt also Eastern Europe, which has the task of preparing the sixth post-Atlantean period. They also use the forces working from the constellation of Sagittarius for this."[175]

In the Mystery Dramas, during the course of his soul spiritual development, Johannes Thomasius (the youth in Goethe's fairytale[176]) experiences a suprasensory encounter with his ahrimanic double and with his luciferic spirit of youth,[177] of which the fiery red centaur in the sketch is an imaginative image. (Rudolf Steiner indicated this role should be played by an actor of Slavic descent.) Thus, the Eastern Slav, with his or her inner disposition for the new etheric clairvoyance,[178] as is evident from the portrayal of this peach-blossom colored figure, is between the luciferic temptation rooted in the astral body (the centaur) and the ahrimanic temptation rising from the depths of the physical being. The two tempters strive, as it were, from opposite sides and for different goals, to master the forces of the person's special etheric body. As the present work has shown in detail,[179] the Western lodges and Jesuit Order also wish to use this particular configuration of the soul–spiritual nature of the Eastern Slavs in their struggle against the legitimate appearance of the spirit self in earthly evolution. The former try to mislead humanity with "Americanism," in which the powers of the double work with special force,[180] while the latter offers one-sided, only spiritual religiosity. The latter easily assumes a fanatical or exalted character and, above all, shies away from concrete knowledge of the spirit, trying to persist with merely vague, purely emotional experiences. (Such an inner attitude would result in the full victory of the Luciferic centaur in the Slavic soul.)

In both cases, significant hindrances would be placed in the path to the spirit self for the Eastern Slavic people, to the point of making it completely impossible to unite with it. This would happen if the ahrimanic forces were able, through the double, to extinguish from outside the light of the spirit self that is arising in the soul, or if the centaur, penetrating in a luciferic way into the soul, was able, through feelings or one-sided religiosity, to darken its original, pure wisdom-filled radiant being. In the sketch, however, not only are these two dangers portrayed, but also the path for overcoming them. And for the Eastern Slav the appropriate path is presented in the image of the cross surrounded by seven red roses. This central symbol of esoteric Christianity points to that power which, when it is developed within the soul on the path of modern Christian-Rosicrucian initiation as contained in Anthroposophy,[181] is capable of protecting the Slavic human being from both of the dangers that lie in wait. (This is the reason that Anthroposophy, as the most important fruit of Central European spiritual development, is so significant for the Slavic human being.[182]) For only with its help will he or she be able not only to withstand the temptations coming from the luciferic air-centaur and the double that is nourished by the dark forces rising from the depths of the Earth, but will also be able to *drive* them *from* his or her own being by the beginning of the sixth epoch. This moment is presented in the sketch: the fire-red centaur climbing upward must abandon the human soul, because it does not have the strength to bear contact with the impulses of esoteric Christianity. Thereby, however, the power of astral energy and one-sided religiosity that it bears within is not lost, but is transformed into the circle of roses around the cross. The circle of roses is an image of the fully purified and clarified astrality[183], and at the same time, in its *sevenfold* nature, it is a symbol of objective, selfless (non-egoistic) spirit knowledge. The luciferic powers have no access to such knowledge. This knowledge transforms itself from a human knowledge ever more into knowledge of the surrounding spiritual cosmos to which he or she belongs and from which he or she originally came. (For this reason, there are seven shining stars in the cupola painting itself, instead of seven roses.)

Moreover, the cross undergoes a significant metamorphosis. From black it becomes a blue, a bearer of the new death-conquering, spiritualized, and spiritually creative Will that proceeds from the consciousness soul and is able to overcome the forces of the ahrimanic double within the human being. "Therefore the Russian will be called to furnish the most important impulses for the age when the double must be finally overthrown: in the sixth post-Atlantean cultural period."[184] In the composition [of the sketch], the crossbeam of the cross is a direct continuation of the gesture of the right hand of the blue angel. Through this the impression arises that it is the angel that has given the transformed cross to the human figure below. In the lecture "What Does the Angel Do in Our Astral Body?"[185] Rudolf Steiner describes how even today beings of the hierarchy of the angels are striving to awake in human souls the three attributes that he characterized, in a somewhat different connection, as being central for the sixth cultural epoch.[186] These three attributes are fraternity, religious freedom, and Spiritual Science. In the sketch ("The Slavic Human"), one can clearly distinguish these three elements evoked by the angels. In the egg-shaped auric form we have an indication of the configuration of the astral body that has developed in itself the forces of brotherhood to the highest degree. For as a high ideal, "there hovers before us this community that will so encompass the sixth cultural period that civilized human beings will meet each other naturally as brothers and sisters."[187] The blue angel inspires the development of this universal human brotherhood of the sixth epoch through the gesture of *both* arms that form a half-circle that reproduces the form of the aura. Daniel van Bemmelen writes in connection with this: "He [the Slavic human] will be helped by the blue angel, that imprints upon his or her astral body the image of brotherhood in social life under the inspiration of the spirit self for the future."[188] However, when the angel's two arms together inspire the future human being of the sixth epoch to brotherhood, individually, they inspire the other two soul attributes mentioned earlier. Thus the raised left hand of the angel that lets the stream of radiant gold flow from upward downward and gradually fill the entire space of the egg-shaped aura is also an image of absolute "religious freedom," or "free religiosity," that will so show itself in the epoch of the spirit self that "all of life will be made into an expression of the suprasensory."[189] Finally, the cross with the seven roses, the symbol of esoteric Christianity, signifies the spreading of Spiritual Science or Anthroposophy on the Earth, which has begun today with the life work of Rudolf Steiner.

In addition, the composition as a whole is an expression of the fivefold human being as he or she will be in the sixth cultural epoch. The dark double connected with the material forces of the Earth and portrayed at the bottom of the sketch is related to the forces of the human *physical* body; the peach blossom color of the figure of the Slavic Human indicates the *etheric body*; the egg-shaped aura around the Slavic Human, the *astral body* (in the sketch it is depicted as being already permeated by the substance of the spirit self), where, however, the centaur lurks as its luciferic counter-image. The cross with the roses is connected with the "I" that reveals itself in the fullness of its forces in the spiritualized consciousness soul. The sources of the substance of the spirit self, however, are depicted in the figure of the blue angel. In conclusion, it should be pointed out that the gesture of the angel with the raised left arm and the right hand stretching downward corresponds to the main gestures of the central figure of the Representative of Humanity as portrayed in the eastern part of the paintings of the small cupola. For according to Rudolf Steiner's spiritual scientific research, Christ has been working in the spiritual environment of the Earth since the Mystery of Golgotha and will continue to do so, especially from the fifth post-Atlantean cultural epoch on—in particular, through the hierarchy closest to the human world, that of the angels.[190] The Slavic human being, the main bearer of the impulses of esoteric Christianity in the sixth cultural epoch, follows this gesture of the angel, the emissary of the Christ, with complete devotion. Hence, he is surrounded in the sketch by the golden (Christ-) aura and is in balance between the fiery red centaur floating upward and the dark double connected with the depths of the Earth (in the paintings of the small cupola, the latter has a dark brown color). And this combination of colors—gold between fire-red and dark brown—corresponds exactly to the range of colors of the central motif of the small cupola: the Representative of Humanity between Lucifer and Ahriman.[191] Thus, the higher destiny of the Eastern Slavic people as Christ-people comes to full expression in this sketch by Rudolf Steiner.

Addendum

Reinhard Piper, Christian Morgenstern's publisher, asked Morgenstern to write an autobiographical text to be included in an almanac to celebrate the publishing company's jubilee. Christian Morgenstern did not wish to do this. "Basically, I do not have in any way the slightest desire to put myself forward with people." However, because Piper would not give up asking, Morgenstern jotted down this list for him:

1871	Birth
1881	Death of my mother
1887	Friederich Kayssler
1894	Beginning of journeys, illness, freedom
1900	Translation of Ibsen's *Brand*
1905	The Gospel of John
1909	My wife
1910	Rudolf Steiner

Bernhard Piper was not satisfied and continued to press him for something longer and more substantial. It is most likely that Christian Morgenstern felt that Reinhard Piper did not understand who he really was. In any case, he then wrote the autobiographical poem below for Bernhard Piper in which he tries to show him that it is the future that is important to him, not the past. All has become new! According to Michael Bauer, Christian Morgenstern did later write the autobiographical text that Bernhard Piper requested.[192]

The full poem follows. The last stanza is quoted in this volume.

For Reinhard Piper

If you want to know who I am,
Look at whom I am becoming.
Beyond the old, which is gone,
humans and the Earth open themselves anew.

Open anew to the new spirit;
let the long dried-up be blessed,
and what it brings and shows us,
shall alone from now on meet us.

Finally, all became new!
The womb of spirit that bore us,
with inexpressible loyalty,
has summoned us back again.

Once again, we ascend
as once we descended.
Once again, a struggle began,
but not to defeat.

And the human being, who stood firmly
and seemed at the end of all knowing,
suddenly sees a world
turn incredibly upward.

Für Reinhard Piper

Wollt ihr wissen, wer ich bin,
mögt ihr künden, wer ich werde.
Über Altem, das dahin,
öffnen neu sich Mensch und Erde.

Öffnen neu sich neum Geist,
lassen lange Dürre segnen;
und was er uns bringt und weist,
soll fortan allein begegnen.

Endlich ward denn alles neu!
Geisterschoß, der uns geboren,
hat uns unaussprechlich treu,
neu zu sich zurückbeschworen.

Wieder steigen wir hinan,
wie wir einst hinabgestiegen.
Abermals ein Kampf began,
doch zu keinem Unterliegen.

Und der Mensch, der sich gestellt
schien an allen Wissens Ende,
sieht auf einmal eine Welt
unerhörter Aufwärtswende.[193]

Notes and References

(*StA = Annotated Stuttgart Edition*)

1 Sergei O. Prokofieff, *Wie stehen wir heute vor Rudolf Steiner?* [in English in Prokofieff and Selg, *Crisis in the Anthroposophical Society*, Forest Row, UK: Temple Lodge, 2013], Arlesheim 2012.

2 Rudolf Steiner, Rudolf Steiner: *Die Konstitution der Allgemeinen Anthroposophischen Gesellschaft und der Freien Hoschschule für Geisteswissenschaft. Der Wiederaufbau des Goetheanum* [The Constitution of the General Anthroposophical Society and the Independent School for Spiritual Science. The reconstruction of the Goetheanum] (GA 260a), Dornach 1987.

3 Compare Sergei O. Prokofieff, *33 Jahre Tatigkeit als anthroposophischer Schriftsteller, 1980–2013* [Thirty-three years' activity as anthroposophical author, 1980–2013], Dornach 2014; and Peter Selg, *The Destiny of the Michael Community*, SteinerBooks 2015.

4 Christian Morgenstern, *Werke und Briefe* [Works and letters], annotated Stuttgart edition (StA), vol. 5, "Aphorisms," Stuttgart 1987.

5 Compare Peter Selg, *Christian Morgenstern. Sein Weg mit Rudolf Steiner* [Christian Morgenstern. His path with Rudolf Steiner], Stuttgart 2013.

6 Christian Morgenstern, *Werke und Briefe* [Works and letters], Annotated Stuttgart Edition (StA), vol. 2. Lyrics 1906—1914. Stuttgart 1992 (from the poem, "Nachts im Wald" [Nights in the forest], in *Melencholie* [Melancholy).

7 Marie Steiner-von Sivers, in Rudolf Steiner: *Christian Morgenstern. Der Sieg des Lebens* über den Tod. [Christian Morgenstern. The victory of life over death]. Dornach 1935.

8 Ibid.

9 Christian Morgenstern, *Werke und Briefe* [Works and letters], annotated Stuttgart edition (StA), vol. 8. Correspondence 1904–1908, Stuttgart 2011.
10 StA, Volume 5, Stuttgart 1987.
11 Rudolf Steiner, *Our Dead: Memorial, Funeral, and Cremation Addresses*, CW 261, SteinerBooks 2011.
12 Rudolf Meyer, *Christian Morgnstern in Berlin*, Stuttgart 1959.
13 Concerning the difficulty the Platonists had to incarnate properly in the nineteenth and twentieth centuries owing to the circumstances of the time, compare Peter Selg, *The Destiny of the Michael Community*, SteinerBooks 2015.
14 Rudolf Steiner: *Our Dead*. CW 261, SteinerBooks 2011.
15 Rudolf Steiner, *Die Kunst der Rezitation und Deklamation* [The art of recitation and declamation], Dornach 1987.
16 Rudolf Steiner, *Our Dead*. CW 261, SteinerBooks 2011.
17 Rudolf Steiner, *Four Mystery Dramas*, CW 14, SteinerBooks 2015.
18 Quoted from Michael Bauer, *Christian Morgensterns Leben und Werk* [Christian Morgenstern's life and work]; completed by Margareta Morgenstern and Rudolf Meyer (with contributions from Friedrich Kayssler), Munich 1933.
19 Ibid.
20 StA, vol. 5. Stuttgart 1987.
21 Ibid.
22 Concerning the relationship of Rudolf Steiner to the individuality of Christian Rosenkreutz and the stream going out from him, compare Peter Selg, *Rudolf Steiner and Christian Rosenkreutz*, SteinerBooks 2012.
23 Letter to Margareta Gosebruch von Liechtenstern on May 15, 1909. In Christian Morgenstern, *Ein Leben in Briefen* [A life in letters], ed. Margareta Morgenstern, Wiesbaden 1952.
24 Ibid.
25 Compare Peter Selg, *Christian Morgenstern. Sein Weg mit Rudolf Steiner* [Christian Morgenstern: His path with Rudolf Steiner], Stuttgart 2013.
26 In Christian Morgenstern: *Ein Leben in Briefen* [A life in letters]. Edited by Margareta Morgenstern. Wiesbaden 1952. (Revised from the handwritten letters).
27 Ibid. (Revised).
28 Ibid.
29 StA, vol. 5, Stuttgart 1987.
30 Rudolf Steiner, "Das Wesen der Anthroposophie" [The nature of Anthroposophy]. Opening lecture of the first General Meeting of

the Anthroposophical Society. Berlin, Feb. 3, 1913; in *Archivemagazin. Beiträge zur Rudolf Steiner Gesamtausgabe* [Archive magazine. Contributions to the Rudolf Steiner collected works] no. 1 (not in the Collected Works).

31 In a letter to Ludwig Sauter in the summer of 1913 Michael Bauer wrote, "None of us can as yet truly comprehend the greatness and extent of his work; we are standing too close." In *Gesammelte Werke* [Collected works], ed. Christoph Rau, vol. 5, Stuttgart 1997.

32 Quoted from Hella Wiesberger, "Christian Morgensterns Lebensbegegnung mit Rudolf Steiner" [Christian Morgenstern's meeting with Rudolf Steiner]; in *Beiträge zur Rudolf Steiner Gesamtausgabe* [Contributions to the Rudolf Steiner collected works], pamphlet no. 33, Easter 1971.

33 StA, vol. 5. The "human being who had come to the end..." refers to Christian Morgenstern himself.

34 Ibid. "... one has done this..." refers to Christian Morgenstern himself.

35 StA, vol. 2. "... the human being..." refers to Christian Morgenstern himself.

36 Quoted from Hella Wiesberger, "Christian Morgensterns Lebensbegegnung mit Rudolf Steiner" [Christian Morgenstern's meeting with Rudolf Steiner], in *Beiträge zur Rudolf Steiner Gesamtausgabe* [Contributions to the Rudolf Steiner collected works], pamphlet no. 33, Easter 1971.

37 StA, vol. 2.

38 In Christian Morgenstern, *Ein Leben in Briefen* [A life in letters], ed. Margareta Morgenstern, Wiesbaden 1952 (revised from the handwritten letters).

39 StA, vol. 5.

40 Rudolf Steiner, *Michaelmas and the Soul-Forces of Man*, CW 223, SteinerBooks 2012.

41 StA, vol. 8.

42 StA, vol. 5.

43 "Meditationen" [Meditations] in StA, vol. 2.

44 Rudolf Steiner, *The Esoteric Aspect of the Social Question*, CW 193, Rudolf Steiner Press.

45 Michael Bauer, "Rudolf Steiner und der Schulungsweg" [Rudolf Steiner and the path of schooling], in *Gesammelte Werke* [Collected works], vol. 4, Stuttgart 1990.

46 Rudolf Steiner, *Wo und wie findet man den Geist?* [Where and how does one find the spirit?], GA 57, Dornach 1984.

47 Rudolf Steiner, *The Evolution of Consciousness,* CW 227, Rudolf Steiner Press 2006.

48 Rudolf Steiner, *Anthroposophy, ihre Erkenntniswurzeln und Lebensfrüchte* [Anthroposophy, the roots of its knowledge and its life fruits; partially translated as *Fruits of Anthroposophy*], GA 78, Dornach 1986.

49 Rudolf Steiner, Reincarnation and Karma, CW 135, SteinerBooks 2001.

50 Ibid.

51 Quoted from B.-U. Kusch, *Christian Morgenstern. Sein Weg zur Anthroposophie* [Christian Morgenstern: His path to Anthroposophy], Freiburg 1982.

52 "An die Mitglieder der Theosophischen Gesellschaft (Deutsche Sektion), den Johannesbau in München betreffend" [To the members of the Theosophical Society concerning the Johannes Building in Munich]; on behalf of the council of the management of the Johannes Building Association. October/November 1911.

53 Quoted from Michael Bauer, *Christian Morgenstern.*

54 Letter to Margareta Morgenstern on Sept. 24, 1912, unpublished; compare Peter Selg, *Christian Morgenstern. Sein Weg mit Rudolf Steiner* [Christian Morgenstern. His path with Rudolf Steiner], Stuttgart 2013.

55 In Michael Bauer, *Gesammelte Werke* [Collected works], vol. 5. "Letters."

56 StA, vol. 2.

57 Letter to Alfred Guttmann on May 25, 1909.

58 Quoted from Michael Bauer, *Christian Morgenstern.*

59 Rudolf Steiner, *Our Dead,* CW 261, SteinerBooks 2011.

60 Sept. 27, 1909, unpublished, Rudolf Steiner Archive in Dornach. Compare Peter Selg, *Christian Morgenstern. Sein Weg mit Rudolf Steiner* [Christian Morgenstern: His path with Rudolf Steiner], Stuttgart 2013.

61 Quoted from Albert Steffen, *Aus Geisteswegen* [From spirit paths], Dornach 1942.

62 Compare Rudolf Steiner, *Vortrâge und Kurse über christlich-religiöses Wirken,* vol. 2, *Spirituelles Erkennen—Religiöses Empfinden—Kultisches Handeln* [lectures and courses on Christian-religious work: Spiritual knowing—spiritual feeling—ritualistic doing, GA 343, Dornach 1993.

63 Rudolf Steiner, *The Human Spirit,* CW 167, Rudolf Steiner Press 2016.

64 StA, vol. 2.

65 In Rudolf Steiner, Christian Morgenstern. Der Sieg des Lebens über den Tod [Christian Morgenstern: The victory of life over death].
66 Rudolf Steiner, *Our Dead,* CW 261, SteinerBooks 2011.
67 Addition from Christian Morgenstern in a letter from Margareta Morgenstern to Rudolf Steiner at the beginning of March 1914, unpublished, Rudolf Steiner Archive in Dornach. Compare Peter Selg, *Christian Morgenstern. Sein Weg mit Rudolf Steiner* [Christian Morgenstern: His path with Rudolf Steiner], Stuttgart 2013.
68 Rudolf Steiner, *Our Dead,* CW 261, SteinerBooks 2011.
69 Ibid.
70 Ibid.
71 Ibid.
72 Rudolf Steiner/Marie Steiner-Von Sivers, *Die Kunst der Rezitation und Deklamation* [The art of recitation and declamation], Dornach 1987.
73 Ibid.
74 Rudolf Steiner, *Our Dead,* CW 261, SteinerBooks 2011.
75 Ibid.
76 Rudolf Steiner, *The Presence of the Dead on the Spiritual Path,* CW 154, SteinerBooks 1990.
77 Rudolf Steiner, *Our Dead,* CW 261, SteinerBooks 2011.
78 Rudolf Steiner, *Esoteric Christianity,* CW 130, Rudolf Steiner Press 2001.
79 Compare StA, vol. 2.
80 Letter with postmark of July 17, 1911, unpublished. Compare Peter Selg, *Christian Morgenstern. Sein Weg mit Rudolf Steiner* [Christian Morgenstern: His path with Rudolf Steiner], Stuttgart 2013.
81 Rudolf Steiner, *Our Dead,* CW 261, SteinerBooks 2011. "He will live among us as model; he will live among us in such manner that when we ask ourselves: How should the best anthroposophist be?—we will answer with one of the first names the name of Christian Morgenstern."
82 Rudolf Steiner, *Die Mission einzelner Volkseelen im Zusammenhang mit der germanisch-nordisch Mythologie* [The mission of individual folk souls in connection with the Germanic-Nordic mythology], CW 121, Dornach 1982.
83 Rudolf Steiner, *Christ and the Human Soul,* CW 155, Rudolf Steiner Press 2008.
84 Rudolf Steiner, *The Presence of the Dead on the Spiritual Path,* CW 154, SteinerBooks 1990.
85 Rudolf Steiner, *Our Dead,* CW 261, SteinerBooks 2011.

86 Rudolf Steiner, *The Presence of the Dead on the Spiritual Path*, CW 154, SteinerBooks 1990.
87 Rudolf Steiner, *Inner Reading and Inner Hearing*, CW 156, SteinerBooks 2008.
88 Rudolf Steiner, *The Presence of the Dead on the Spiritual Path*, CW 154, SteinerBooks 1990.
89 StA, vol. 2.
90 Rudolf Steiner, *The Presence of the Dead on the Spiritual Path*, CW 154, SteinerBooks 1990.
91 Rudolf Steiner, *Wege der geistigen Erkenntnis und der Erneuerung künstlerischer Weltanschauung* [Ways of spiritual knowledge and the renewal of the artistic worldview], GA 161, Dornach 1999.
92 Rudolf Steiner, *Christian Morgenstern. Der Sieg des Lebens* über *den Tod* [Christian Morgenstern: The victory of life over death], Dornach 1935 (not in the Collected Works).
93 Rudolf Steiner, *Approaching the Mystery of Golgotha*, CW 152, SteinerBooks 2006.
94 Ibid.
95 In Rudolf Steiner, *Christian Morgenstern. Der Sieg des Lebens* über *den Tod* [Christian Morgenstern: The victory of life over death], Dornach 1935 (not in the Collected Works). Sergei O. Prokofieff wrote in *The Mystery of the Resurrection in the Light of Anthroposophy*, "Not only the knowledge of the human being could he [Christian Morgenstern] bring to the souls in spirit land, but it was this knowledge itself, that filled his whole being and rayed out from him into the spiritual world." Sergei O. Prokofieff to pointed out the special relationship of Christian Morgenstern—since the Ascension—the presence of the Sun forces of Christ present in the human etheric body. Morgenstern could, according to Prokofieff, through his "unique connection to the depths of the anthroposophic Christology," strengthen extraordinarily the Christ-force in his etheric body and was, because of this, able "to carry with him into the spiritual world after death his entire individualized, thoroughly experienced and thoroughly felt anthroposophical knowledge" (Ibid.).
96 Rudolf Steiner, *Wege der geistigen Erkenntnis und der Erneuerung künstlerischer Weltanschauung* [Ways of spiritual knowledge and the renewal of the artistic worldview], GA 161, Dornach 1999.
97 Rudolf Steiner, *Inner Reading and Inner Hearing*, CW 156, SteinerBooks 2008.
98 Compare Rudolf Steiner, *Esoteric Christianity*, CW 130, Rudolf Steiner Press 2001.

99 Rudolf Steiner, *Christ and the Human Soul,* CW 155, Rudolf Steiner Press 2008.

100 Ibid.

101 Rudolf Steiner, *Christian Morgenstern. Der Sieg des Lebens* über *den Tod* [Christian Morgenstern: The victory of life over death], Dornach 1935 (not in the Collected Works).

102 Rudolf Steiner, *Our Dead,* CW 261, SteinerBooks 2011.

103 Rudolf Steiner, *Christian Morgenstern. Der Sieg des Lebens* über *den Tod* [Christian Morgenstern: The victory of life over death],. Dornach 1935 (not in the Collected Works).

104 Rudolf Steiner, *Christ and the Human Soul,* CW 155, Rudolf Steiner Press 2008.

105 Rudolf Steiner, *The Presence of the Dead on the Spiritual Path,* CW 154, SteinerBooks 1990.

106 Rudolf Steiner, *Our Dead,* CW 261, SteinerBooks 2011.

107 Rudolf Steiner, *Christian Morgenstern. Der Sieg des Lebens* über *den Tod* [Christian Morgenstern: The victory of life over death], Dornach 1935 (not in the Collected Works).

108 Ibid.

109 Letter to Rudolf Steiner at the beginning of March 1914, Rudolf Steiner Archive in Dornach. Compare Peter Selg, *Christian Morgenstern: Sein Weg mit Rudolf Steiner* [Christian Morgenstern: His path with Rudolf Steiner], Stuttgart 2013.

110 Rudolf Steiner; Address for Sept. 20, 1914; in *Christian Morgenstern. Der Sieg des Lebens* über *den Tod,* Dornach 1935 (not in the Collected Works).

111 Rudolf Steiner, *Christ and the Human Soul,* CW 155, Rudolf Steiner Press 2008. Compare also among others Andreas Neider, *Christus-Impuls und Rosenkreutzertum. Rudolf Steiners Weg zum Fünften Evangelium* [Christ-impulse and Rosencrucianism. Rudolf Steiner's path to the *Fifth Gospel*], Stuttgart 2012.

112 Rudolf Steiner, Address for Sept. 20, 1914, in *Christian Morgenstern. Der Sieg des Lebens* über *den Tod,* Dornach 1935 (not in the Collected Works).

113 StA, vol. 2. Compare also the editorial commentary there: "Single page, handwritten (in the Rudolf Steiner Estate Administration, Dornach. May 2–3, 1912; handwritten copy by Margareta M. in the Estate, with the note: TO R. St. and dated May 13, 1912." (Ibid.). Therefore, Rudolf Steiner had in his edition of *We Have Found a Path* the original from Christian Morgenstern ("written in pencil in Christian Morgenstern's beautiful handwriting"), but

it seems he took the date of the verse as given on Margareta Morgenstern's copy.

114 Rudolf Steiner, *The Presence of the Dead on the Spiritual Path,* CW 154, SteinerBooks 1990.

115 Marie Steiner-von Sivers, in Rudolf Steiner, *Christian Morgenstern. Der Sieg des Lebens* über *den Tod,* Dornach 1935 (not in the Collected Works).

116 Ibid.

117 StA, vol. 2.

118 Ibid.

119 Ibid.

120 Ibid.

121 Ibid,

122 Ibid.

123 Ibid.

124 Quoted from Christoph Rau, *Michael Bauer: Sein Leben und sein Begegnung mit Friedrich Rittelmeyer* [Michael Bauer: his life and his meeting with Friedrich Rittelmeyer], Dornach 1995.

125 Quoted from Margareta Morgenstern, *Michael Bauer. Ein Bürger beider Welten* [Michael Bauer: A citizen of both worlds], Stuttgart 1950.

126 In *Gesammelte Werke* [Collected works], vol. 5.

127 Margarita Woloschin, *The Green Snake: An Autobiography,* Floris Books 2010.

128 Friedrich Rittelmeyer, "Michael Bauer," in *Die Christiangemeinschaft* [The Christian Community], 1929.

129 Alexander Strakosch, *Lebenswege mit Rudolf Steiner. Erinnerungen* [Life paths with Rudolf Steiner: Memories], Dornach 1994.

130 In *Gesammelte Werke* [Collected works], vol. 2.

131 Compare Peter Selg, *Michael Bauer. Ein esoterischer Sch*üler Rudolf Steiners [Michael Bauer: An esoteric pupil of Rudolf Steiner], Dornach 2006.

132 In *Gesammelte Werke* [Collected works] Vol. 4.

133 Quoted from Michael Bauer, *Christian Morgenstern.*

134 Ibid.

135 Ibid.

136 Ibid.

137 Ibid. Also in his letter to Bruno Cassirer on Nov. 7/8, 1907, Morgenstern stressed the "love for life that could be called almost religious in all of life's manifestations" as an element of Russian art and culture (StA, vol. 8).

138 Ibid.

139 Christian Morgenstern, *Ein Leben in Briefen* [A life in letters].

140 Compare, concerning this, the summarized, and continuing presentations by Sergei O. Prokofieff, *The Spiritual Origins of Eastern Europe and the Future Mysteries of the Holy Grail*, Temple Lodge 1993.

141 Published in Rudolf Steiner, *Our Connection with the Elemental World*, CW 158, Rudolf Steiner Press 2017; addresses of Apr. 11, 1912 and June 5, 1913.

142 Ibid.

143 Ibid.

144 Ibid.

145 Ibid.

146 Ibid.

147 Ibid.

148 Ibid.

149 Rudolf Steiner, *Die Kunst der Rezitation und Deklamation* [The art of recitation and declamation], GA 281.

150 Andrei Bely, *Verwandeln des Lebens. Erinnerungen an Rudolf Steiner* [Transformation of life: Memories of Rudolf Steiner], Basel 1977.

151 Michael Bauer, *Christian Morgenstern*.

152 Compare Rudolf Steiner, "What Does the Angel Do in Our Astral Body?"; Oct. 9, 1918, in *Death as Metamorphosis of Life*, CW 182, SteinerBooks 2008.

153 Michael Bauer, *Christian Morgenstern*.

154 Rudolf Steiner, *Our Connection with the Elemental World*, CW 158, Rudolf Steiner Press 2017.

155 In Sergei O. Prokofieff, *The Spiritual Origins of Eastern Europe and the Future Mysteries of the Holy Grail*, Temple Lodge 1993.

156 Quoted from Hilde Raske, *The Language of Color in the First Goethanum: A Study of Rudolf Steiner's Art*, Walter Keller Verlag, Dornach (English ed. undated).

157 See Rudolf Steiner, *How to Know Higher Worlds*, CW 10, SteinerBooks 1994.

158 About the fact that the sixth epoch will have a clairvoyant character, see Rudolf Steiner, *The Challenge of the Times*, CW 186, SteinerBooks 1979 (Dec. 7, 1918). "One can also say that just as the human 'I' achieves a consciousness of itself through the 'image-apparatus' of the physical body, so, too, will the human 'I,' imbued with spirit self, be able to serve as such an 'image apparatus' for the etheric body in the sixth epoch. Through this the possibility will open up for it to behold the processes and beings of the astral

world consciously, just as it can see the processes and beings of the physical world today" (Sergei O. Prokofieff).

159 Compare Rudolf Steiner, *Our Connection with the Elemental World,* CW 158, Rudolf Steiner Press 2017.

160 "That the astral (soul) aura of the Slavic human being is depicted in the sketch is also confirmed through the following fact. In the book *Theosophy* (CW 9) Rudolf Steiner writes, 'With different people the size of this aura is different. Yet one can—on average—somewhat imagine that the entire human being appears twice as tall and four-times as wide as the physical' (in "Thought Forms and the Human Aura," *Theosophy,* SteinerBooks 1994)—"When one expands the figure of the 'Slavic Human Being'—that is depicted only to the waist—to its full size, then in height it is only half as large and in the width only one-quarter of the astral egg" (Sergei O. Prokofieff).

161 Compare Rudolf Steiner, *Colour,* CW 291, Rudolf Steiner Press 1997.

162 Rudolf Steiner, *Our Connection with the Elemental World,* CW 158, Rudolf Steiner Press 2017. (lect. Nov. 9, 1914). Compare Sergei O. Prokofieff, *Eternal Individuality: Towards a Karmic Biography of Novalis,* Temple Lodge 1992, ch. 6 and 7.

163 Rudolf Steiner, *Die Mission der neuen Geistesoffenbarung* [The mission of the new spiritual revelation], GA 127, Dornach 1989. Compare Rudolf Steiner, *Theosophy,* CW 9, SteinerBooks 1994 ("Body, Soul and Spirit").

164 Compare lecture of Feb. 23, 1905, in Rudolf Steiner, *Goethes geheime Offenbarung in seinem Mârchen von der grünen Schlange und der schönen Lilie* [Goethe's secret revelation in his fairytale of the green snake and the beautiful lily], Dornach 1982.

165 Ibid.; Feb. 16, 1905.

166 Ibid.; Feb. 23, 1905. About the meaning of the bright yellow and gold colors in the human aura, Rudolf Steiner writes in , *Theosophy,* "Thought Forms and the Human Aura": "Bright *yellow* appears here when the thinking is filled with high, comprehensive ideas that the individual grasps from the whole divine world order. This yellow then has, when the thinking is intuitive and is purified of sense impressions, a *golden sheen.*"

167 Rudolf Steiner, *The Challenge of the Times,* CW 186, SteinerBooks 1979 (Dec. 8, 1918).

168 Rudolf Steiner, *Secret Brotherhoods,* CW 178, Rudolf Steiner Press 2004 (Nov. 16, 1917).

169 Rudolf Steiner, *Building Stones for an Understanding of the Mystery of Golgotha,* CW 175, Rudolf Steiner Press 2015.

170 See the lecture of May 29, 1921, in the separate edition in 1986 with the title, *Der Baugedanke des Goetheanums* [The building-idea of the Goetheanum].

171 See concerning this, for example, Rudlof Steiner, *Anthroposophy and the Inner Life,* CW 234, Rudolf Steiner Press 2015.

172 Compare Rudolf Steiner, *Our Connection with the Elemental World,* CW 158, Rudolf Steiner Press 2017 (Apr. 11, 1912).

173 Ibid.

174 Rudolf Steiner, *Secret Brotherhoods,* CW 178, Rudolf Steiner Press 2004 (Nov. 16, 1917).

175 Ibid.

176 Compare Rudolf Steiner, *Entwürfe, Fragmente und Paralipomena zu den vier Mysteriendramen* [Sketches, fragments and margin-notes for the *Four mystery dramas*], GA 44.

177 The meetings of Johannes Thomasius with his double take place in the second, third, and fourth dramas, with the spirit of his youth taking place in the fourth. Compare Rudolf Steiner, *Four Mystery Dramas,* CW 14, SteinerBooks 2015.

178 Compare Sergei O. Prokofieff, *The Spiritual Origins of Eastern Europe and the Future Mysteries of the Holy Grail,* Temple Lodge 1993 (ch. 20: "The Spiritual Destiny of Eastern Europe in the Light of the Karma of Humanity").

179 Ibid.

180 Rudolf Steiner, *Secret Brotherhoods,* CW 178, Rudolf Steiner Press 2004 (Nov. 16, 1917).

181 Compare Rudolf Steiner, *An Outline of Esoteric Science,* CW 13, Anthroposophic Press 1997; "Knowledge of Higher Worlds: Initiation," as well as lecture of June 6, 1907, in Rudolf Steiner, *Rosicrucian Wisdom,* CW 99, Rudolf Steiner Press 2006.

182 "There is a salvation for Russia; there is salvation, but this salvation may not be sought on a false path. Moreover, I do not say this because I love Theosophy, but because the whole evolution of humanity can teach us that as the truth. There is a salvation for Russia, and this salvation is called: theosophy. For other regions of the Earth theosophy will be extraordinary and will bring humanity forward. For Russia, theosophy will be the only salvation. It is what must be there so that the Russian folk finds its connection to its folk soul, so that this folk soul will not be called to other tasks in the world than the one that is predetermined for it"

(Rudolf Steiner, *Our Connection with the Elemental World,* CW 158, Rudolf Steiner Press 2017).

183 See Rudolf Steiner, *Outline of Esoteric Science,* CW 13, Anthroposophic Press 1997 ("Knowledge of Higher Worlds: Initiation"). "To the origin of the roses there point the red rays from the transformed and purified forces of the centaurs; the red rays that ray down from their feet to the roses" (Sergei O. Prokofieff).

184 Rudolf Steiner, *Secret Brotherhoods,* CW 178, Rudolf Steiner Press 2004 (Nov. 16, 1917).

185 Rudolf Steiner, *Death as Metamorphosis of Life,* CW 182, SteinerBooks 2008 (Oct. 9, 1918).

186 Rudolf Steiner, *Das Geheimnis des Todes. Wesen und Bedeutung Mitteleuropas und die europäischer Volksgeister* [The mystery of death: Nature and significance of Central Europe and the European folk spirits], GA 159 (June 15, 1915). See Sergei O. Prokofieff, *Eternal Individuality: Towards a Karmic Biography of Novalis,* Temple Lodge 1992, ch. 7, "The Forerunner of the Sixth Cultural Epoch."

187 Rudolf Steiner, *Das Geheimnis des Todes. Wesen und Bedeutung Mitteleuropas und die europäischer Volksgeister* [The mystery of death. Nature and significance of Central Europe and the European folk spirits], GA 159, Dornach 2005.

188 Daniel van Bemmelen, *Rudolf Steiners farbige Gestaltung des Goetheanums* [Rudolf Steiner's color-form of the Goetheanum], Stuttgart 1973, ch. 4.

189 Rudolf Steiner, *Death as Metamorphosis of Life,* CW 182, SteinerBooks 2008 (Oct. 9, 1918). In the same lecture Rudolf Steiner said that, when this stage in the evolution of humanity has been reached, "the Church," as an earthly institution, "when it correctly understands itself, can have only the one intention, and that is to make itself unnecessary on the physical plane."

190 Rudolf Steiner, *The Spiritual Guidance of the Individual and Humanity,* CW 15, SteinerBooks 1992, ch. 3; also Rudolf Steiner, *Approaching the Mystery of Golgotha,* CW 152, SteinerBooks 2006 (May 2, 1913).

191 "Also the following color relationships are full of significance. In the pastel sketch of the middle motif of the eastern small cupola: in 'The Representative of Humanity between Lucifer and Ahriman,' the figure of Christ as the representative of the higher 'I' (spirit self) is gold. It is surrounded, however, by a peach-blossom-colored aura in the form of an egg. That means it is depicted with an etheric vestment. In contrast, the Slavic human in the sketch is the color

of peach blossom; this means, gifted with clairvoyance, with the natural ability to perceive this etheric vestment of Christ. And the Slavic human is surrounded by a powerful astral aura that is filled with the gold sheen of the spirit self. For in the sixth Epoch the human being will not live in the spirit self as in his or her 'I'—that will happen first on the Jupiter evolution—but from outside, surrounded by it like a blessed higher aura shining down upon him or her *from above* (as is shown in the sketch)" (Sergei O. Prokofieff).

192 Compare Peter Selg, *Christian Morgenstern. Sein Weg mit Rudolf Steiner* [Christian Morgenstern: His path with Rudolf Steiner], Stuttgart 2013.

193 In StA, vol. 2; see also Peter Selg, *Christian Morgenstern. Sein Weg mit Rudolf Steiner*, Stuttgart 2013.

Books in English Translation by Peter Selg

On Rudolf Steiner

Rudolf Steiner: Life and Work: *(1923): The Burning of the Goetheanum*, vol. 6 of 7 (2018)

Rudolf Steiner: Life and Work: *(1919–1922): Social Threefolding and the Waldorf School*, vol. 5 of 7 (2017)

Rudolf Steiner: Life and Work: *(1914–1918): The Years of World War I* , vol. 4 of 7 (2016)

Rudolf Steiner: Life and Work: *(1900–1914): Spiritual Science and Spiritual Community*, vol. 3 of 7 (2015)

Rudolf Steiner: Life and Work: *(1890–1900): Weimar and Berlin*, vol. 2 of 7 (2014)

Rudolf Steiner: Life and Work: *(1861–1890): Childhood, Youth, and Study Years*, vol. 1 of 7 (2014)

Rudolf Steiner and Christian Rosenkreutz (2012)

Rudolf Steiner as a Spiritual Teacher: *From Recollections of Those Who Knew Him* (2010)

On Christology

The Sufferings of the Nathan Soul: *Anthroposophic Christology on the Eve of World War I* (2016)

The Lord's Prayer and Rudolf Steiner: *A Study of His Insights into the Archetypal Prayer of Christianity* (2014)

The Creative Power of Anthroposophical Christology: *An Outline of Occult Science · The First Goetheanum · The Fifth Gospel · The Christmas Conference* (with Sergei O. Prokofieff) (2012)

Christ and the Disciples: *The Destiny of an Inner Community* (2012)

The Figure of Christ: *Rudolf Steiner and the Spiritual Intention behind the Goetheanum's Central Work of Art* (2009)

Rudolf Steiner and the Fifth Gospel: *Insights into a New Understanding of the Christ Mystery* (2010)

Seeing Christ in Sickness and Healing (2005)

On General Anthroposophy

The Anthroposophical Society: *The Understanding and Continued Activity of the Christmas Conference* (2018); with Marc Desaules

The Warmth Meditation: *A Path to the Good in the Service of Healing* (2016)

The Michael School: *And the School of Spiritual Science* (2016)

The Destiny of the Michael Community: Foundation Stone for the Future (2014)

Spiritual Resistance: *Ita Wegman 1933–1935* (2014)

The Last Three Years: *Ita Wegman in Ascona, 1940–1943* (2014)

From Gurs to Auschwitz: *The Inner Journey of Maria Krehbiel-Darmstädter* (2013)

Crisis in the Anthroposophical Society: *And Pathways to the Future* (2013); with Sergei O. Prokofieff

Rudolf Steiner's Foundation Stone Meditation: *And the Destruction of the Twentieth Century* (2013)

The Culture of Selflessness: *Rudolf Steiner, the Fifth Gospel, and the Time of Extremes* (2012)

The Mystery of the Heart: *The Sacramental Physiology of the Heart in Aristotle, Thomas Aquinas, and Rudolf Steiner* (2012)

Rudolf Steiner and the School for Spiritual Science: *The Foundation of the "First Class"* (2012)

Rudolf Steiner's Intentions for the Anthroposophical Society: *The Executive Council, the School for Spiritual Science, and the Sections* (2011)

The Fundamental Social Law: *Rudolf Steiner on the Work of the Individual and the Spirit of Community* (2011)

The Path of the Soul after Death: *The Community of the Living and the Dead as Witnessed by Rudolf Steiner in his Eulogies and Farewell Addresses* (2011)

The Agriculture Course, Koberwitz, Whitsun 1924: *Rudolf Steiner and the Beginnings of Biodynamics* (2010)

On Anthroposophical Medicine and Curative Education

Honoring Life: *Medical Ethics and Physician-Assisted Suicide* (2014); with Sergei O. Prokofieff

I Am for Going Ahead: *Ita Wegman's Work for the Social Ideals of Anthroposophy* (2012)

The Child with Special Needs: *Letters and Essays on Curative Education* (ed.) (2009)

Ita Wegman and Karl König: *Letters and Documents* (2008)

Karl König's Path to Anthroposophy (2008)

Karl König: My Task: *Autobiography and Biographies* (ed.) (2008)

On Child Development and Waldorf Education

The Child as a Sense Organ: *An Anthroposophic Understanding of Imitation Processes* (2017)

I Am Different from You: *How Children Experience Themselves and the World in the Middle of Childhood* (2011)

Unbornness: *Human Pre-existence and the Journey toward Birth* (2010)

The Essence of Waldorf Education (2010)

The Therapeutic Eye: *How Rudolf Steiner Observed Children* (2008)

A Grand Metamorphosis: *Contributions to the Spiritual-Scientific Anthropology and Education of Adolescents* (2008)

Ita Wegman Institute
for Basic Research into Anthroposophy

Pfeffinger Weg 1a, ch 4144 Arlesheim, Switzerland
www.wegmaninstitut.ch
e-mail: sekretariat@wegmaninstitut.ch

The Ita Wegman Institute for Basic Research into Anthroposophy is a non-profit research and teaching organization. It undertakes basic research into the lifework of Dr. Rudolf Steiner (1861–1925) and the application of Anthroposophy in specific areas of life, especially medicine, education, and curative education. Work carried out by the Institute is supported by a number of foundations and organizations and an international group of friends and supporters. The Director of the Institute is Prof. Dr. Peter Selg.

A Note from SteinerBooks

SteinerBooks is a 501(c)(3) not-for-profit organization, incorporated in New York State since 1928 to promote the progress and welfare of humanity and to increase public awareness of Rudolf Steiner (1861–1925), the Austrian-born polymath writer, lecturer, spiritual scientist, philosopher, cosmologist, educator, psychologist, alchemist, ecologist, Christian mystic, comparative religionist, and evolutionary theorist, who was the creator of Anthroposophy ("human wisdom") as a path uniting the spiritual in the human being with the spiritual in the universe; and to this end publish and distribute books for adults and children, utilize the electronic media, hold conferences, and engage in similar activities making available his works and exploring themes arising from, and related to, them and the movement that he founded.

- We commission translations of books by Rudolf Steiner unpublished in English, as well as new translations for updated editions.
- Our aim is to make works on Anthroposophy available to all by publishing and distributing both introductory and advanced works on spiritual research.
- New books are published for both print and digital editions to reach the widest possible readership.
- Recent technology also makes it efficient for us to make our previously out-of-print works available for the next generation.

SteinerBooks depends on our readers' financial support, which is greatly needed, appreciated, and tax-deductible. Please consider a donation by check or other means to SteinerBooks, 610 Main St., Great Barrington, MA 01230. We accept donations via PayPal at www.steinerbooks.org. For more information about supporting our work, send email to friends@steinerbooks.org or call 413-528-8233.